THIS WAY TO THE REVOLUTION

Art, activism and upheaval
in Birmingham 1968

© Ian Francis, 2019
All rights reserved. This book or any portion thereof may not be reproduced or used in any manner whatsoever without the express written permission of the publisher except for the use of brief quotations in a book review.

ISBN: 978-1-52723258-7

Design by: Justin Hallström
Front cover image:
Rally in Victoria Square, 5 May 1968, by Nick Hedges

Printed by BALTOprint in Vilnius, Lithuania

Excerpt from 'The Journey Back' by Abdullah Hussein (1981) reproduced by permission of Oxford University Press, Pakistan
Lyrics for 'Enoch Power' (1971) reproduced by permission of Millie Small

Published by:
Flatpack Projects
304, The Custard Factory
Gibb Street, Digbeth
Birmingham B9 4AA
United Kingdom

Flatpack Projects is a Charitable Incorporated Organisation
Registered Charity Number: 1162754

www.flatpackfestival.org.uk

Dedicated to Chris Upton and Pete James

CONTENTS

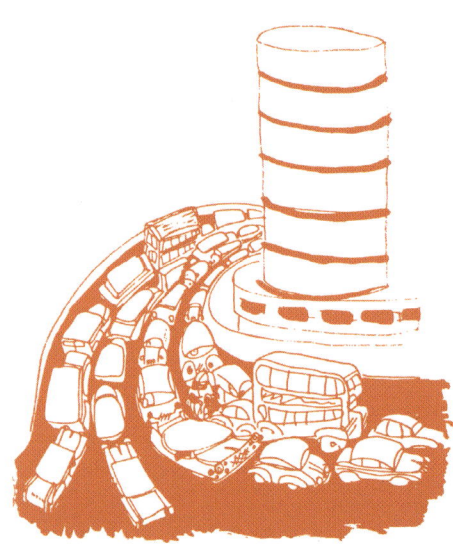

"I have never been very certain as to the value of tangible links with the past. They are often more sentimental than valuable... As for future generations, I think they will be better occupied in applying their thoughts and energies to forging ahead, rather than looking backward."

– Herbert Manzoni, 1957

Rotunda cartoon (Wormzy, 1968)

08 Building a City of the Future
12 Timeline & Key Locations
18 Two Americans in Birmingham
26 One Kind of Life
34 Steve Ajao
36 Festival Arts
38 Asian Teenager
44 Work Is A Four Letter Word
46 Ghost Streets of Balsall Heath
54 Less Than Nothing
62 This Is Our Lab - Let's Not Get Busted
72 Mothers Days
78 The Big Bear Ffolly
86 The Birmingham Inner Circle
94 Black and White Unite and Fight
100 The Journey Back
102 Occupation Tonight!
110 Miracles Take A Little Longer
118 I Can't Find Brummagem
120 Enoch Power
122 Forward
130 Epilogue: Frank and Val

134 Thanks
136 Images
138 Further Reading
140 Index

BUILDING THE CITY

In 1970, The International Times ran a hitch-hiker's guide to the UK which gave short shrift to the second city. "Essentially, Birmingham is a drag. Avoid it if possible, the centre being a trifle confusing to a stoned freak and the suburbs hostile and impossible to navigate." Disorientating and disconnected, it seemed like the kind of place which might require signposts directing you to the revolution. By that point, had the sixties even reached Birmingham?

OF THE FUTURE

As it turns out, they had - but in a very particular form. The international climate of 1968 is well-documented and heavily mythologised: uprisings, occupations, assassinations, and a countercultural youth movement which rejected outright the values of the preceding generation ("don't trust anyone over 30"). What I found interesting was the way these wider battles translated into the context of a sprawling Midlands city experiencing its own dual revolution. Firstly, a radical, decade-long reshaping of core areas which displaced whole communities and saw the creation of a new ring road. Secondly, a growth in the migrant population as workers from across the world arrived in numbers to take up less popular jobs in industry, health and construction.

All of this came together for me in Balsall Heath, a couple of miles south of Birmingham city centre. I've lived in the area half my life, but I didn't really understand its history until I was introduced to a box full of photographs taken here by American student Janet Mendelsohn in 1968. These images of forgotten shops, bomb-sites and people triggered a flurry of amateur detective work, which gradually snowballed to incorporate student protests, immigration policy, back-street art collectives and a bizarre Cilla Black film shot in Ladywood. I became convinced that this turbulent period played a big part in shaping the Birmingham that we know today.

In spring 2018 the Flatpack Festival programme included a weekend of events devoted to this time - from a vicar-led biker cafe in a Digbeth church to a psychedelic club above a furniture shop, from a lost radio programme about Asian teenagers to a mass occupation of university buildings. After this the real work began, with a team of volunteers scattering across the city to gather some of the stories that emerged from the festival. These in turn made their way into a series of podcasts, and the book that you are holding.

The blueprint for the New Birmingham was laid out in a series of articles in the Evening Mail in 1959, written by Frank Price. Price was a local councillor who had risen quickly through the ranks to become Chair of the Public Works Committee, a role with a significant amount of influence over road-building and planning in Birmingham. Since the 1930s the city had been grappling with a proliferation of poor quality slum housing in central areas, and a lack of separation between industrial and residential areas which made living conditions unbearable for some. By the late 1950s it was estimated that over 30,000 families would require rehousing, with many more on the waiting list.

The plan to address these issues - and a projected fourfold increase in traffic - had been conceived before the war by City Engineer Herbert Manzoni. Unsentimental about old buildings and keen to implement a bold solution rather than fiddling around the edges, Manzoni mapped out a scheme for five 'new towns' and a ring road system which would transform the face of the city. He found a committed, pugnacious ally in Price, who had himself grown up in a back-to-back in Hockley and wanted to shake off his hometown's reputation for overcrowding, pollution and squalor. Research trips to Europe and the US helped to refine the plan, and the Evening Mail articles are full of references to the envious world beyond. "What Birmingham does today, the country does tomorrow... the sociologists, town planners and representatives of peoples from all parts of the globe applaud what is now being done."

Birmingham would indeed become an object of fascination and study during the sixties, not just for its experiments in redevelopment but also as a test-case in the emerging field of race relations. By 1966 overseas immigrants accounted for 11% of the city's population (from just under 5% in 1951), of which around half were from Commonwealth countries - in particular the Caribbean and the Indian subcontinent. There was still a relative abundance of unskilled employment at the more menial end of manufacturing as well as in construction, healthcare and transportation. On the other hand, places to live were at a premium, and given that you needed to be a local resident for five years in order to qualify for a council home the majority of overseas workers ended up in privately-rented, multi-occupancy accommodation in the city's inner and middle rings.

Housing had become a focal point for indigenous resentment towards non-white immigrants - most notoriously in Smethwick, just beyond the city's western boundaries in Sandwell. In 1964 Conservative candidate Peter Griffiths became the new MP following a campaign which explicitly played on racial tensions, also refusing to condemn leaflets produced by Colin Jordan's National Socialist Movement which used the slogan "If you want a nigger for a neighbour, vote Labour." The following year Malcolm X made a brief visit to Smethwick a few days before his murder, invited by the Indian Workers' Association. His influence would continue to resonate for activists of colour in Birmingham, helping to inspire a more militant, less integrationist approach as the decade progressed.

Along with redevelopment and racial politics, the other principal ingredient in our story is a youth culture shaped by young people themselves. So many baby-boomers that we interviewed talked about a sense of possibility - that a new world was at hand, and that they could play a part in building it. Tumultuous changes in Birmingham's landscape and its demographics helped to open up fissures and gaps, and through these gaps sprouted new life. The question that inspired this project was "why did so many things begin in 1968?" Whether motivated by a utopian impulse or a survival instinct, this seems to have been one of those punk-like moments when people took it upon themselves to open a venue, start a band, launch a movement. *This Way to the Revolution* attempts to trace the evolution of some of these DIY endeavours, join the dots between them, and investigate the marks that they left behind.

The New Birmingham (Frank Price, 1960)

A REVOLUTIONARY YEAR

THE WORLD

30 JANUARY

Vietnam's National Liberation Front launches The Tet Offensive, a series of surprise attacks that would see them temporarily occupy a number of strategic locations including the US Embassy in Saigon.

17 FEBRUARY

20,000 protestors from around the world gather in West Berlin for the International Congress on Vietnam, organised by Students for a Democratic Society.

4 MARCH

After taking power early in 1968, reformist Czechoslovakian prime minister Alexander Dubček announces the abolition of censorship, signalling the beginning of a thaw in Soviet control known as the Prague Spring.

4 APRIL

Dr Martin Luther King is assassinated at the Lorraine Hotel in Memphis, Tennessee. Riots erupt in cities across America, lasting for several days.

BIRMINGHAM

17 JANUARY

A large sit-in at Aston University begins in opposition to the suspension of six students who had failed their exams. It was one of the first of many such protests that would sweep across campuses in the late sixties.

21 FEBRUARY

Radio 4 broadcast a two-part programme called *Asian Teenager*. Produced in Birmingham by Charles Parker and narrated by Stuart Hall, the show features a range of views from young British Asians in Southall and the West Midlands.

4 FEBRUARY

Thousands of Sikhs hold a silent march through Wolverhampton in protest against a ban on bus-drivers wearing turbans.

31 MARCH

The Carlton Ballroom, a club above a furniture shop in Erdington, promotes a performance by the Freddie Mack Sound under the banner of 'Mothers'. By August the Carlton has completely rebranded as Mothers, catering to a growing audience for blues, rock and psychedelia with acts including Pink Floyd, Muddy Waters and Soft Machine.

23 APRIL

The Race Relations Bill receives its second reading in the Houses of Parliament, while over a thousand London dockers go on strike and march to Westminster in support of Enoch Powell.

6 MAY

In the wake of the closure of Nanterre and Sorbonne campuses by university authorities in response to student occupations, 20,000 people march in Paris demanding that charges are dropped and the buildings reopened. Within a few days protests have snowballed with over a million taking to the city's streets, and by the following week ten million French workers are on strike.

16 MAY

A kitchen gas explosion on the 18th floor causes the partial collapse of Ronan Point, a tower block in Newham, East London. Four people are killed, and seventeen injured.

7 JUNE

A group of women sewing machinists walk out of the Ford plant in Dagenham in protest at pay inequality.

---

20 APRIL

Enoch Powell speaks at the General Meeting of the West Midlands Area Conservative Political Centre in the Midland Hotel on New Street. A response to the proposed Race Relations Act which passes into law six months later, Powell's address becomes known as the 'Rivers of Blood' speech.

5 MAY

Prime Minister Harold Wilson gives a speech at Birmingham Town Hall, intended as a direct riposte to Powell. Outside in Victoria Square British nationalists clash with a protest organised by the Indian Workers' Association.

27 APRIL

West Bromwich Albion beat Birmingham City 2-0 in the FA Cup semi-final at Villa Park. The Baggies go on to win the Wembley final against Everton, followed by a chaotic victory parade between New Street Station and West Brom Town Hall on 19 May.

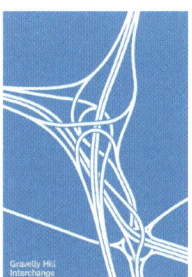

1 JUNE

The phrase 'spaghetti junction' is coined by the Evening Mail, describing the recently-unveiled plans for a major interchange on the M6 motorway at Gravelly Hill. Construction begins in the summer, completing in 1972.

TIMELINE

21 AUGUST

Half a million troops enter Czechoslovakia as part of the Soviet-led Warsaw Pact invasion, marking the end of the Prague Spring.

26 AUGUST

The Democratic National Convention gets underway in Chicago, the scene of several violent clashes between police and anti-war demonstrators throughout the week.

7 SEPTEMBER

The women's liberation movement pickets the Miss America beauty pageant in Atlantic City, New Jersey, an early landmark in second-wave feminism.

20 JULY

Singer Robert Plant performs a gig with the band Obstweedle at Birmingham Teacher Training College. In the audience is guitarist Jimmy Page, who asks Plant to be part of a new group eventually known as Led Zeppelin.

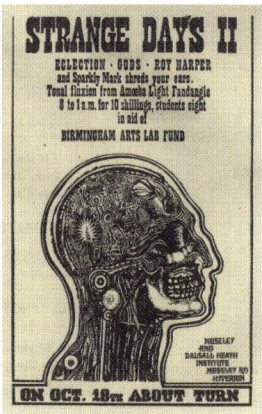

8 SEPTEMBER

Five young members of the Midlands Arts Centre meet to discuss a breakaway endeavour which would in early 1969 become the Birmingham Arts Lab in Tower Street, Newtown. Several months of fundraising events under the name Strange Days follow, with acts including Fleetwood Mac, Colosseum and John Peel.

16 SEPTEMBER

A blues-rock four-piece from Aston play one of their first gigs under the name Earth, at the newly established Henry's Blueshouse on Hill Street in Birmingham. Venue promoter Jim Simpson becomes the band's manager, and within a few months they rename themselves Black Sabbath after a Mario Bava horror film.

5 OCTOBER

A civil rights march in Derry is batoned off the streets by the Royal Ulster Constabulary, resulting in two days of serious rioting across the city.

16 OCTOBER

During the medals ceremony for the men's 200 metres at the Mexico Olympics, athletes Tommie Smith and John Carlos raise their fists in a Black Power salute.

22 NOVEMBER

'The White Album' by the Beatles comes out in the UK. The following fortnight sees the release of *Astral Weeks* by Van Morrison, *The Village Green Preservation Society* by The Kinks and *Beggar's Banquet* by The Rolling Stones.

19 DECEMBER

Lindsay Anderson's debut feature *If...* is released in British cinemas, the tale of a public school uprising which distils the tumult of 1968.

2 OCTOBER

Sheila Thorns from Selly Oak gives birth to Britain's first set of sextuplets at Birmingham Maternity Hospital, with 28 medical staff present. Only three of the babies survive the year.

27 NOVEMBER

A large-scale occupation begins at the University of Birmingham's Great Hall, in protest at the lack of student representation in university decision-making. Students vote to end the occupation at a mass gathering on 5 December.

1 DECEMBER

The first nationwide conference of Black Youth, an offshoot of the Black Power movement, takes place at Birmingham Town Hall. Speakers include Tariq Ali, Roy Sawh and Mihir Gupta.

KEY LOCATIONS

1. Carlton Ballroom, Erdington High St, Erdington
   Site of the legendary Mothers club
   from 1968-1971 (p72)

2. Lodge Road, Aston
   Birthplace of Ozzy Osborne, lead singer of
   Black Sabbath (p78)

3. Tower Street, Newtown
   Location for the Birmingham Arts Lab
   from 1969-1977 (p62)

4. Victoria Square, Birmingham city centre
   Site of the Black and White Unite and Fight
   rally, 5 May 1968 (p94)

5. St Basil's Church, Heath Mill Lane, Digbeth
   Hosted the Double Zero club from 1966 till it
   closed in 1971, and then became home to
   St Basil's youth homelessness charity (p54)

6. Five Ways, Ladywood
   Principal location for 1968 film *Work Is A Four
   Letter Word* (p44), and just down the road from
   where Frank Cook grew up (p22)

7. Marshall Street, Smethwick
   On the invitation of Avtar Singh Jouhl,
   in February 1965 Malcolm X visited here in
   the wake of Peter Griffiths' notorious
   election campaign (p11)

8. Clevedon Road, Balsall Heath
   Many of Janet Mendelsohn's photographs were
   taken within a few blocks of this street (p46),
   just a few minutes walk from the
   Midlands Arts Centre (p26)

9. University of Birmingham, Selly Oak
   Site of the Centre for Contemporary Cultural
   Studies from 1964 to 2002 (p20), and of the Great
   Hall student occupation which took place in the
   winter of 1968 (p102)

TWO AMERICANS IN BIRMINGHAM

When Janet Mendelsohn and Richard Rogers arrived in Birmingham in the autumn of 1967, the redevelopment juggernaut had been in motion for almost a decade. The soaring flyovers and tower-blocks of the new Birmingham had been built from an American template so in some ways they would have felt right at home, but there was still plenty of evidence of the Victorian metropolis, industrial grime and wartime hardship which the city was so keen to leave behind. The couple had graduated from Harvard and crossed the Atlantic to enrol at the groundbreaking Centre for Contemporary Cultural Studies, then based in a temporary cabin on the campus at Birmingham University.

Janet Mendelsohn and Richard Rogers (Richard P Rogers, 1968)

CCCS was established in 1964 by Richard Hoggart, author of *The Uses of Literacy*. Hoggart had used his own Leeds childhood as a basis to study the growing influence of mass media, and one of his ambitions for the Centre was to establish popular culture as a legitimate area for academic research. Funded in part by Penguin Books - grateful to Hoggart for his role as defence witness in the 1960 *Lady Chatterley's Lover* obscenity trial - the Centre's first appointment was that of Stuart Hall in the role of deputy director. Jamaican-born and a Rhodes scholar at Oxford, Hall was founding editor of the New Left Review and had already been developing a form of cultural studies through his teaching at Chelsea College. He would not officially become director of CCCS until 1972, but by the late sixties he had already played a vital part in shaping its approach: porous boundaries between teaching staff and students; an emphasis on collaborative projects; and a strong element of practice-based research with students encouraged off campus to explore the city around them.

This last aspect would have helped draw Rogers and Mendelsohn to Birmingham. Along with sociology he had studied photography as an undergraduate, while she had experimented with the medium as part of her degree in Social Relations. Rogers spent the summer before they left the US filming a group of young people at their hangout spot in an abandoned quarry above Quincy, Massachusetts, with Mendelsohn helping out on sound. Later edited into a short, impressionistic documentary called *Quarry*, this footage contained in embryonic form the approach which the couple would adopt in Birmingham. Subjective and intimate in the vein of Danny Lyons' biker gang portraits, we see teenagers diving, drinking and making out, while the soundtrack interweaves bubblegum pop with taped reflections on parents, love, work and the draft.

Loading a roll of film at their Edgbaston flat, Janet Mendelsohn took a snapshot of her bookshelves which gives us some idea of what they were reading at the time. Alongside French cookery books and student guides to Europe and swinging London, there's plenty that would have been on the syllabus at CCCS. *The Parliamentary Leper* is a memoir by Birmingham's first Asian councillor Dhani Prem, and *Race, Community and Conflict* is an influential study of one Birmingham neighbourhood by two sociologists, John Rex and Robert Moore, which looked at the intersection of housing policy and racial tensions in Sparkbrook. The couple also brought a North American perspective to these questions, informed by books like Kenneth Clarke's *Dark Ghetto* and Kevin Lynch's *The Image of the City*: "what does the city's form mean to the people who actually live there?" Perhaps most important in terms of the shape their finished work would take is *A Fortunate Man*, a collaboration between John

Above:
Catherine and Stuart Hall
(Richard P Rogers, 1968).

Below:
Campus map
(CCCS Annual Report, 1966-67).

Opposite:
Alexander Street, Ladywood
(Richard P Rogers, 1968).
Clevedon Road, Balsall Heath
(Janet Mendelsohn, 1968)

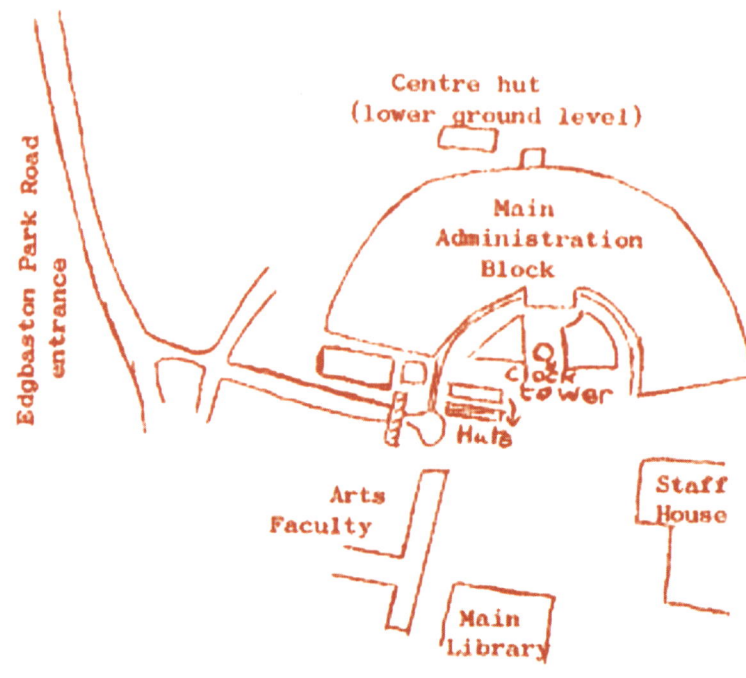

KASHMIR
COFFEE BAR
RUBBER & PLASTICS MANUFACTURERS
HIGH WYCOMBE AND AT NORTHAMPTON

Berger and Jean Mohr combining text and photography to reflect on the life of a country doctor.

By the end of the year each had selected a central 'character' for their study and a specific neighbourhood, both part of the redevelopment plan but distinct in a number of ways. Janet Mendelsohn worked a stone's throw from home in Balsall Heath, best known as Birmingham's red light district and since the 1920s a place where newcomers to the city would touch down - whether European Jewish, Irish, Afro-Caribbean or more recently South Asian. She became particularly close to one sex-worker, photographing her, her boyfriend and her children, while also documenting the shops and cafes around them and the 'bomb-pecks' which acted as alluringly hazardous adventure plagrounds. Her images capture a sense of transition - both in terms of the area's fluid cultural mix and the streets themselves, many of them ear-marked for demolition in a couple of years.

A mile north-east, the bulldozers had already been busy. Predominantly white and working-class, by 1968 a significant strip of Ladywood had been flattened to make way for the middle ring road and new council housing. Richard Rogers followed budding artist Frank Cook back to his family home in Alexander Street, a boarded-up terrace where his parents were one of the last to be moved out. Frank and his wife Val had themselves recently relocated to Balsall Heath, and Frank had taken on some studio space down the road at the new Midlands Arts Centre for young people. Rogers followed their trajectory from back-to-backs to bohemian bedsits, along the way recording the way a new youth culture was taking shape not just at the centre but at parties and protests across the city.

Although activism isn't directly addressed in either study, it was a background hum throughout this period. Influenced by student actions in America, France and Germany the previous year, a wave of campus occupations spread across the UK during 1968. Locally Aston University was the first to catch the bug in January, and then in June students at Birmingham College of Art refused to take their exams in opposition to the assessment regime. The University of Birmingham was a little slower to catch on, but already that spring there were glimmers of dissent. Stuart Hall and a group of graduates and undergraduates edited an edition of the university magazine Mermaid which attacked the hierarchical, conformist character of academia, and in June Hall led an outdoor 'teach-in' to protest a visiting lecture by Enoch Powell. In the autumn CCCS would become an unofficial nerve-centre for the occupation of the university's Great Hall, mobilising both staff and students and making use of the centre's Gestetner machine to crank out leaflets and posters.

By this point Rogers and Mendelsohn had moved on to the Royal College of Art in London. The fruits of their Birmingham research wouldn't appear in

> "Miss Janet Mendelsohn and Mr. Richard Rogers are exploring the use of photography as a tool of cultural analysis and field work. These studies will also make use of tape-recorded interviews and field notes. Special attention will be paid to such elements as theme, narrative, layout and sequence as ways of structuring a photographic essay."
>
> – CCCS annual report, 1967

V: What time are you coming home tonight?
F: *About half past two.*
V: Oh, Frank I've got to get up at half past seven tomorrow morning.
F: *I don't care what you have to do, your working has nothing to do with me.*
V: It is. I can't go home unless you come with me. I'm not going all that way on my own.
F: *It's nothing to do with me. I don't care what your sleeping habits are.*
V: It's not my sleeping habits, it's just that I've got to go out to work so as to get you money to buy your paint.
F: *You haven't given me any paint.*
V: I have.
F: *My painting is totally independent.*
V: You don't have to get up at half past seven in the morning. I do.
F: *I'm not asking you to get up at any hour; I'm just telling you that I'm not coming home.*
V: But Frank, the reason that I have to get up at half past seven is to go to work and earn money.
F: *So what?*
V: Well you don't.
F: *I don't recently.*
V: Therefore you should come home with me.
F: *It's a good bit of strategy to bend my life the way you want it.*

Frank and Val Cook (Richard P Rogers, 1968)

print until early 1969, when another university magazine Alta featured two photo stories: 'Varna Road' by Janet Mendelsohn and 'Frank Cook' by Richard Rogers. The first is a blunt, bleak snapshot of prostitution and family, with testimonies from 'A Girl's Mother', 'A Girl' and 'Her Pimp'. The second is a typically sixties tale of social mobility, with Frank describing his journey from Ladywood via grammar school to the Arts Centre and on to Chelsea School of Art. It also features a deliciously uncomfortable exchange between Frank and Val highlighting the tensions between nine-to-five and an artist's life.

Mendelsohn and Rogers split up around this time, but after they returned to the US they would continue to collaborate on occasional projects - including *Neighbors*, a 1977 film about the renewal of a Boston district which examined the human costs of gentrification. Their UK work disappeared from view, until in 2014 the University of Birmingham mounted an exhibition and symposium to mark fifty years since the establishment of CCCS. The centre had been closed down amid some acrimony in 2002, and in some ways this was an attempt to build bridges with former students and staff including Stuart Hall. Kieran Connell in the university's history department tracked down Janet Mendelsohn, who retrieved two boxes of photographs and negatives from her basement in Massachusetts and donated them to the project, which in turn led to a major exhibition of the Varna Road prints at Ikon Gallery. Nearly half a century after she first explored the streets of Balsall Heath, Mendelsohn returned to find a city discovering her photographs for the first time.

Richard Rogers died in 2001 but his wife, documentary photographer Susan Meiselas, also donated copies of the Frank Cook images and contact sheets to the university. The two collections between them amount to over 5,000 images, and they were the catalyst for this project. Although Birmingham was well photographed at that time - including iconic work by Vanley Burke, Paul Hill and Nick Hedges (p86) - by spending months with their respective subjects these two Americans left us with a uniquely intimate outsiders' view of a city in flux. Largely limiting herself to a few blocks, Janet Mendelsohn expressed a potent sense of one particular neighbourhood and the connections she formed with the people she met. If there is a little more distance in Richard Rogers' images, there is also a wider canvas. Frank and Val moved freely around the city, and in their wake Rogers captured clues that would become part of our story: a pair of DJs at a basement disco; a traveller family on wasteland; a poster for a club called Mothers; a DZ patch on a leather jacket.

Val Cook and her mother-in-law walking through Balsall Heath, with poster advertising Fleetwood Mac's upcoming appearance at Mothers club visible on the right. (Mothers Days, p74)

Traveller family on Sherbourne Road site, with newly built Highgate tower block in the background. (Ghost Streets of Balsall Heath, p46)

Mark Williams and Tony Jones at a Midlands Arts Centre music event, germ of the Strange Days gigs which would in turn lead to the Birmingham Arts Lab. (This Is Our Lab, p62)

Detail of a biker's jacket, including Double Zero patch. (Less Than Nothing, p54)

All images by Richard P Rogers, 1968

"It wasn't two lives, it was one kind of life, it was one stance to two things, one stance to a hundred, just me against whatever I was up against."

– Frank Cook, talking to Richard Rogers in 1968

ONE KIND

"On the site of a former Corporation rubbish dump in Cannon Hill Park, the most ambitious arts centre in the country is being created. Along the banks of the Rea, bounded by the cricket ground, the slums of Balsall Heath, the police college and the Tally-Ho tennis club, they are building a vast emporium of the arts, a Battersea Fun Fair of the elevated faculties."

– Alan Shuttleworth, Mermaid 1967

OF LIFE

Along with football games, picnics and condemned terraces, a number of Richard Rogers' images show Frank Cook working at his studio in the Midlands Arts Centre. At the time the MAC (as it is now known) was still a work in progress taking shape next to a lake in an Edgbaston park. As well as the visual arts department, these photographs record the daily life of the new building: music rehearsals, pottery workshops, chess games and discos. The entire facility was designed for the under-25s, and Rogers happened to be visiting at a crucial moment when the vision of the place was being stress-tested by a new generation willing to question everything around them.

The Centre's director John English had resigned his post as an industrial chemist at Chance Glass Works after the war, in order to pursue a passion for community theatre which spawned Wolverhampton's Arena Theatre company and the Highbury Theatre in Sutton Coldfield, as well as numerous touring shows in parks across the region. During this period he and his wife Mollie Randle conceived the notion of a permanent arts centre for young people, drawing up a proposal which won the patronage of councillor Frank Price. In 1962 Birmingham City Council donated eight acres of Cannon Hill Park to the project on a peppercorn rent, and by 1964 the first buildings of the then Ardencote Arts Centre were ready to open their doors.

English was adept at extracting finance and support from industrialists and politicians, and expounded at length in the media on his belief that leisure time for most people would only continue to increase, that we must move beyond 'work-think' in order to produce happy and productive citizens. The idea was a bold one, and very much an emblem of Birmingham's mid-sixties confidence. Although a good deal of public and private investment was ploughed into the centre in its early years, the plan was always that subscription fees would sustain it in the long term. By 1968 facilities included a studio theatre, gallery, café, artists' studios and an outdoor arena, and membership was rising annually. The late artist Bob Groves was a founder of Ikon Gallery and headed the centre's visual arts department that year: "As soon as you stepped inside you were involved in what they were doing. Some of the kids there were wonderful, really terrific. They were doing their own thing - whatever took their fancy."

Images of the Midlands Arts Centre, including Frank Cook - preceding page - and Ian Gorin, below (Richard P Rogers, 1968)

As a working-class boy Frank Cook was not alone, but it's fair to say that he was in a minority. After spending the early part of his life in an Erdington orphanage, Ian Gorin had been raised by relatives in Small Heath and got a place at King Edwards: "We were the first generation that had gone to grammar school from that background. Everybody was bright, everybody was inquisitive, everybody wanted to learn." His wanderlust was stoked by reading Aldous Huxley and the Beats, and as soon as he had the opportunity he began to travel: hitchhiking up and down the M1, sleeping on the streets of Tangiers, hunting for work on Icelandic trawlers. (The

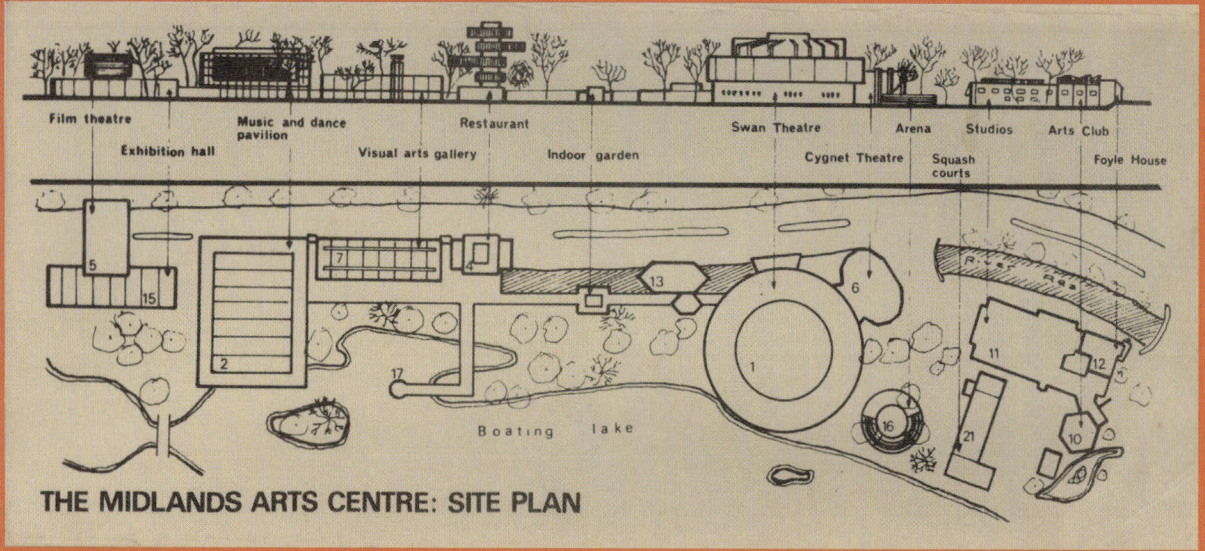

THE MIDLANDS ARTS CENTRE: SITE PLAN

"I like to think of the Midlands Arts Centre as part of the second Industrial Revolution, as a bit of social engineering, an exercise in social cultural education, and this is truly what it is."

John English in 'The Pacemakers', 1969

Planning for a new kind of world

The world we live in is changing rapidly. Everywhere there are new houses and flats, new shopping centres, new schools, new roads, new offices and factories.

The way we live is changing, too. Less of our time has to be spent at work, earning a living; more of our time is free to be with our friends and families, doing the things we choose.

These trends will undoubtedly continue. By the time our children are grown up they will have even greater opportunities for leading a full, rich life.

In this new pattern there should be a natural place for the arts — for music, theatre, painting, sculpture, literature and poetry. Yet these things are unfamiliar to many people, and so they often remain unexplored.

There is no reason, however, why our children should be denied the pleasures and challenges of the arts, along with all the other opportunities which will be theirs. We can plan now to ensure that they have the chance to find out about these things.

The Cannon Hill Trust has been founded to encourage young people to enjoy and practise the arts.

On a carefully chosen site in Cannon Hill Park, the Trust is building theatres for plays, opera, ballet, puppets, and film; pavilions for music and dance;

Promotional leaflet and scale model (Midlands Arts Centre, 1972/1965)

jumper pictured here was picked up in Reykjavik.) Back home he took on a series of jobs including construction work on the new Castle Vale estate - for local company Bryant, who were doing very nicely out of the high-rise boom - while writing songs and performing. It was music that first led him to the Arts Centre.

"I didn't go there with any intention of doing anything in particular, I just went to have a look... I mean, coming from Small Heath it was another planet. This was a place for the Edgbaston bourgeoisie." And yet it was the closest that Gorin had known to a sense of family, and the creative process helped to blur the boundaries: "The thing that brings you together is your love of what you're doing, which is the whole point. So where you're from comes last." He became part of a thriving youth drama setup led by Paul Clements - who went on to set up Contact Theatre in Manchester - and formed a small gang of mates including the underground illustrator Edward Barker. For a time the centre was a genuine home from home, a place to sleep the night for weeks at a stretch with the security guard turning a blind eye: "It was two years of pure freedom; nobody even knew we were there. We were like the Borrowers."

The building's architectural drawings had been populated by serious youngsters with cropped hair and smart clothes, but by the late sixties the climate was very different and John English's bow-tie and talk of social engineering had become increasingly incongruous. One of the MAC's first brushes with the counterculture was the 'Perception Weekend' in late 1967, a visit by Yoko Ono which included a screening of her *Film no.4* (featuring 365 pairs of buttocks) and a 'Be-In' in the outdoor arena on Sunday afternoon including a symbolic attack on a watch borrowed from a member of the audience. "Violently," replied civil engineering student Les Stokes, when asked by The Birmingham Post if he minded his watch being used in this way: "It was worth about £10." There was a minor kerfuffle later on when Ono's manager Tony Cox announced that all were welcome at the weekend's concluding discussion, but English insisted that people must pay for their tickets as advertised. "Everybody was feeling very free and happy after the Be-In," grumbled playwright David Yallop, "and now we come back to the commercial aspect."

The most significant counter-reaction came in the summer of 1968 when a group of dissatisfied young members decided to set up their own Arts Lab, explicitly defined against "the boarding school atmosphere and overt authoritarianism of the Arts Centre" (see p62). English claimed this as a healthy by-product of the work they were doing, and there's plenty of evidence that simply by offering young Brummies a place to connect and experiment he was responsible for an explosion of creativity: examples include symphonic rockers Bachdenkel, who recorded their first tracks there, the scratchy, satirical work of Barker, whose influential cartoons would go on to appear in the NME and The Observer, and the enduring phenomenon of Festival Arts (p36) which started life as a group of friends at the Centre.

Rumblings continued throughout the autumn, with reports of school groups walking out of an unexpurgated MAC production of *Little Malcolm And His Battle With The Eunuchs* directed by a young Tony Robinson, and things finally came to a head during a snowbound February 1969. An international festival of student drama arrived at the Centre as part of a wider arts programme organised by Birmingham University students, including invited companies from Switzerland, Germany and Poland. Guild president Ray Phillips had been a key figure in the recent occupation of the university's Great Hall and remembers that the European guests were disappointed to discover that the protests were over. It's fair to say that they brought with them an atmosphere of insurrection. Robinson, who would go on to prominence with the likes of *Blackadder* and *Time Team*, later recalled the effect they had on the place:

"To show their contempt for us, these young revolutionaries stole Twix bars from the canteen, smoked in the non-smoking area, and walked across the flower beds. Their plays were mostly performed naked, and they poured red paint over the stage which was very hard to get off. The local hippies and sixth-formers who usually inhabited the centre fled in the face of this righteous wrath, but I was intoxicated by it. Of course I disapproved when they drew hammers and sickles on the reception desk with their felt-tip pens, and declined to flush the bowl when they'd been to the lavatory, but I'd never seen such fearless devilry... After they'd gone, the Arts Centre reverted to normal. The shiny wood was re-sanded, waxed and polished, the toilets flushed and the flower beds replanted. But the young anarchists left a hole in my life. Ever afterwards the MAC seemed tame. I missed their righteous anger, the smell of their Gauloises and their acres of pubic hair."

At the epicentre of the trouble was a group from Cologne with an avowed belief in "the complete absence of a system of society." Their nudity and paint-throwing was catnip for the local and then national press, and the Centre found itself with a bona fide media storm on its hands, helped along by irate councillor Nora Hinks demanding John English's resignation and providing pithy quotes: "Birmingham is becoming a decadent city... a sink of iniquity." This episode takes up a significant chunk of the MAC cuttings file, along with a comprehensive internal report which makes no attempt to hide English's exasperation with the anarchists. "During Thursday afternoon members of the Cologne group came to the Centre and attempted to argue with the Director about his decision... In making the point that their performance had not been offensive, several of the Cologne students again removed all their clothing."

The Arts Centre had a tough job reconciling the conservative views of its stakeholders with the less-than-deferential attitudes of its membership and visiting artists, and it's no surprise that programming began to shift in emphasis towards under-seventeens - in the view of the Arts Lab fundraisers at the time, "possibly because they question the system less than the older members." For Ian Gorin, times were definitely changing. Shortly after he was caught distributing weed in the toilets, he and four friends including Barker were informed that their memberships were to be suspended.

Below: Perception Weekend brochure (Midlands Arts Centre, 1967)

Opposite: The Scene That 'Shocked' The City (Redbrick, 26 February 1969)

Perception Weekend with Yoko Ono

BIRMINGHAM UNIVERSITY NEWSPAPER

REDBRICK

No. 758 WEDNESDAY, FEBRUARY 26th. 1969 PRICE 3d.

In Redbrick TODAY

Paris: The political situation now .... Page 3
Roland Chaplain and the Observatory — An Enquiry .... Page 4
Festival: in retrospect .... Page 5
Chicago: the other second city .... Page 6
Reviews: Roland Kirk, 'Gone With The Wind,' John Williams .... Page 7
12.30 a.m.: Measure for Measure cancelled.

THE SCENE THAT 'SHOCKED' THE CITY

A major row has blown up in the local and national press over two incidents during the Drama Festival at Cannon Hill Arts Centre.

The row which has sprung up between Birmingham city officials, the Midland Arts Centre and the Guild has been taken up not only by the Birmingham press but by most of the national daily papers. The controversy is a result of two plays during the International Student Drama Festival at Cannon Hill last week. In the late night performance on Tuesday the German group as part of their performance stripped off and threw paint at each other, and on Wednesday, again in a late-night performance, the Swiss group went through the motions of sexual intercourse in their play. These two isolated incidents were seized upon by the press, resulting in much adverse publicity, both for the Drama Festival, and for Festival itself.

Nude storm: 'Shut Art Centre'

STUDENTS IN FRESH ROW OVER 'SIEGE'

Festival facing big loss

On Monday a "Times" story was headlined "Nudity at arts centre brings protests"; a "Daily Telegraph" headline ran "Inquiry into student 'strip act' sought"; and the "Daily Mail" said "Students' 'sex on stage' starts inquiry."

By PETE DONOVAN

Cologne University students in their performance last Tuesday night

Photo: Eric Sanderson

PATRICK WALL TO SPEAK

At the invitation of the University Conservative Association, Patrick Wall, M.P. for Haltemprice, is to visit the Union on Friday week. On previous visits to universities Major Wall has been the subject of violent protest demonstrations; at Leeds last year

APPEAL – BUT TODAY'S MEETING GOES ON

ROLAND CHAPLAIN announced on Friday that he will be appealing to University Council against his dismissal reported in "Redbrick" last week. He has had an interview with the University Secretary, and at a meeting of Guild Executive on Monday he said that he was confident that Council would institute a full inquiry.

By JOHN KEETLEY

Roland Chaplain

Alan Booth writes: P.S

Teach-in concessions

AFTER a 2½-hour struggle yesterday, the University authorities have made considerable concessions to the Guild over the format of the University Symposium, to be held on March 15th/16th. The argument occurred at a meeting of the Sympmposium Steering Comittee at which Ray Phillips and Clare Dutton asked the University Authorities to make a change in the plans, which they considered too structural and establishmentarian.

Cecylia Lichtig, a member of the Polish Mime Troupe

Above: Life drawing class
(Richard P Rogers, 1968)

Below: Ajao family Christmas,
Ladywood 1958

STEVE AJAO

Almost half a century to the day after Richard Rogers showed a selection of his photographs at the Midlands Arts Centre, Flatpack launched a small exhibition of the same work in the same place. Most of it had been hidden away for the intervening years, and we hoped that in the process of revealing them Frank Cook himself might come to light. By the end of the show we had connected a number of faces to names, and one of these was Steve Ajao - shown here aged 16 in a life drawing class in early 1968. Steve was familiar to me through the south Birmingham music scene, and when I emailed him the image he responded immediately: "Ah yes, I remember that suede jacket."

It turned out that Steve's journey had been similar to Frank's in some ways. His father had emigrated from Nigeria after the war ("come back to the mother country to help rebuild it") and met his mother at a dance - both were keen music-lovers. Steve's infancy was spent in a succession of lodging houses, his parents separating at one point under the strain of life as an inter-racial couple, until 1954 when the council offered the family a back-to-back house on Stour Street in Ladywood. Here the memories are vivid of narrow entry-ways, outdoor toilets, air-raid shelters, coal cellars and the washhouse, Steve sharing the attic room with his sister and one particularly bad winter when the whole courtyard filled with snow: "it was just like an ice field across to somebody else's attic window."

The neighbourhood was also pock-marked with bomb damage, Victorian terraces punctuated by craters of rubble, and in the early 1960s the bulldozers began to move in. "The first transformation I can remember was just waking up one morning hearing a pounding going on outside the window... there was a guy demolishing the air raid shelter immediately outside our house entrance, standing on the top with a sledgehammer and just battling away at it. I mean, those things were built to withstand Hitler's bombs and there's this big Irish navvy with a sledgehammer and he took it away in a day." In the meantime Steve's creative instincts were being nourished at his local primary school, where he was given the leeway to paint vast murals in the main hall. Then he passed his 11-plus, won a place at Moseley School of Art, and a whole new world opened up: "It was like moving out of a black and white movie into colour."

Along with a traditional arts education in lithography, sculpture, perspective and the like, Steve's love of music was also given free rein. "There were one or two guys who had got this guitar that would be passed around in the lunch hour. It had an old vandalised telephone mouthpiece taped under the strings, and the lead of that was taken and connected to the wires of the school record player, so it was like having an amplifier on the other end of this thing." Steve had been exposed to blues and jazz from an early age, and was playing in his dad's band at weekends from the age of thirteen. Suddenly this upbringing had a social cachet in the context of the British blues boom, and at the same time figures like Muhammad Ali and James Brown offered inspiration: "I felt empowered by that... Yeah, no more of this getting shoved around by knuckleheads. I'm glad I lived through that sort of revolution."

Towards the end of his time at school there was a class trip to Paris in the spring of 1968, a "glorified piss-up" where he encountered twitchy gendarmes and had a tour of Picasso's old studio. The riots erupted just as they were boarding the ferry home. Around the same time he began to take art classes at the MAC, which struck him as terribly modern: "like the party scene in *Blow Up*." It was part of an ongoing search for kindred spirits which eventually led him to study fine art at Lanchester Polytechnic, and on weekends home from Coventry he traced the progress of the redevelopment. "You could stand at the top of Aston and look across all the way to Digbeth and just see nothing. It was just acres and acres of nothing, like a Martian landscape.

Programme cover
(Festival Arts, 1969)

1971 King Lear puppet
(David Rowan, 2018)

THIS WAY TO THE REVOLUTION

FESTIVAL ARTS

During the summer of 2019, a volunteer-run theatre company marked fifty years of performing for residents and holiday-makers in the UK's smallest city, St Davids, on the Welsh coast. Festival Arts was the brainchild of Joye and Jack Beckett, two Birmingham teachers who had been part of the early post-war development of schools drama. Their daughters Jenny and Julie were involved from an early age, attending youth camps in Wales - where they met young Americans facing the draft - then later taking part in theatre workshops at MAC and the Birmingham Rep. It was the latter, known as Theatre 67, where Jenny and her boyfriend Colin Baines put together *Conflict*, advertised as "a provocative evening of poems and music." Jack decided to help them develop this into something more substantial, and in the summer of 1969 the same group of Brummie teenagers built a temporary theatre in a garden in St Davids where they performed their anti-war variety show for friends, family and nonplussed locals.

In that first year a programme handout described Festival's ambition "to 'transplant' young people from city environments to a very lovely area in which they can share the arts they have worked to produce throughout the year." The format has changed very little in the intervening fifty years. On Wednesday evenings a group meet at Selly Oak Methodist Church to rehearse two plays, one of them by Shakespeare, and then in July the whole company decamps to Pembrokeshire to perform an intense three-week run of shows. In the early sixties Jack had watched his kids playing in the ruins next to St Davids Cathedral. He noticed the clarity of the acoustics there and thought it would be a perfect place to put on theatre. For Festival's second season in 1970 the company did exactly that, and the Bishop's Palace has been the home for their Shakespeare show every summer since.

Talking to Jenny and Julie - now a teacher and a producer on *The Archers* respectively - it's clear that late sixties ferment played a big part in the birth of Festival, along with the generosity of their parents. "From the minute we started *Conflict*, teenagers would descend upon us to rehearse in the garden at the back. They gradually started staying the night; our house was a sort of hub." This carried over to St Davids too, an annual ritual with its own songs and language. Julie: "They have to wash up together, they have to help with the cooking, they have to run the box office, they have to help with the costume and they have to learn their lines and they have to put a show on. And there's something about that... that is bigger than all those bits."

Festival Arts at the Garden Theatre, 1969. Includes Colin Baines on guitar and Jenny Beckett (later Baines) on the right.

Jack Beckett died in 1986, midway through preparations for a show. Joye had always been the engine-room of the operation and kept it going through a difficult period, continuing to churn out costumes and props. "She wanted to know the shows by March at the latest," remembers Julie, "then she'd be sewing through till August." On being awarded an MBE in 2005, Joye responded: "Festival has been my life's work." Following her death in 2017, the fiftieth season became a tribute to her. Now the daughters have adopted the roles their parents once played, and the company keeps taking it one year at a time. Julie: "We've always said we're not going to hand this over like a curse." Jenny: "If it stops, it stops. I'm left with a shed full of props and a room full of costumes."

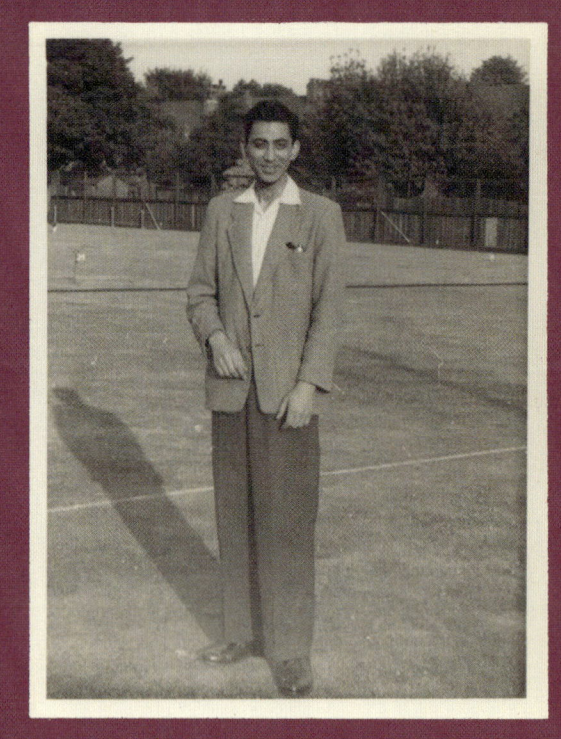

Dilip Hiro, c.1959

ASIAN TEENAGER

"This is Radio 4, the Home Service. We present 'English People Are Not Eating Chapatti!', the first of two programmes on the Asian Teenager, introduced by Stuart Hall, with readings by John Harris, and compiled by Dilip Hiro from conversations recorded with Indian and Pakistani teenagers growing up in the Britain of the 60s..."

So began a 30-minute documentary broadcast on 21 February 1968, a montage of words and music pieced together at BBC Birmingham by producer Charles Parker and editor Mary Baker. Parker was recognised for a uniquely creative approach to the medium forged on the 'Radio Ballads', a series of programmes made between 1958 and 1964 which blended folk music and oral testimony to shed light on subjects including the miner, the boxer, the traveller and the road-builder. It had been some time since he had been allowed to make anything that ambitious or expensive, but on a tighter leash Parker continued to explore ways to experiment with radio and give a voice to the voiceless. The seeds for *Asian Teenager* had been sown the previous summer, thanks to an article in New Society by journalist Dilip Hiro.

Born in Larkana in what was then united British India, during Partition Hiro and his family moved to a refugee colony across the new border in Ulhas Nagar. The young man's dreams of the West were nourished by Somerset Maugham and Hollywood movies, and after taking an engineering degree in Pune he arrived in the UK in November 1957, following an arduous three-week journey from Bombay to Marseille confined to a hammock in fourth class steerage. Keen to avoid being caught in London's expat "Indian cocoon", Hiro took work at engineering firms in Stockton-on-Tees and Kingston-upon-Hull where he met fellow left-wingers, and at the Stockton Palais de Danse discovered the wonderful world of English dating.

After a period working in the USA - "studying the effects of advanced capitalism" - Hiro returned to London in the mid-sixties determined to leave engineering behind and make it as a novelist. Having witnessed the electrifying effect of the civil rights movement and Black Power back in America, he now saw a degree of militancy and turbulence beginning to pierce the veneer of what were then described as 'race relations' in the UK. While trying to adapt his own experiences into fiction the writer began to tout for journalistic work, and one of his first published pieces was an article for Tribune about the London visit of activist Stokely Carmichael. Around this time he was living in Acton and making regular visits to the growing Asian community in Southall ("a small Punjab"). The interviews which he gathered there and in Birmingham formed the basis for 'The Young Asians of Britain', an article in the 1 June 1967 issue of New Society which started Charles Parker thinking about a radio documentary on the same subject.

Hiro had visited his cousin in Birmingham ten years previously - "it was pure Dickens; cold, dark, depressing" - and on arriving at New Street again he was struck by the changes underway in the city centre. "It was very familiar to me having spent some time in Baltimore - they were copying the American model." In the BBC canteen Parker railed against the insipid nature of British cuisine, and impressed Hiro with his fervour. "Charles' background was very middle-class - he grew up in Surbiton, his father worked in insurance and so on. He discovered Marx late in life, and then he went all out." They agreed to develop a two-part series for broadcast in the new year, drawing on and widening the pool of interviewees who had contributed to the article.

The first part focussed on religion, education and history while the second, 'Too Shy In These Matters', was concerned with movies and music, adolescence and sexual mores. At the time media rhetoric was dominated by questions of integration, population statistics and various controversies over housing and employment, so it was unusual to hear young British Asians reflecting on the tensions they had to navigate each day between their parents' values and those of the host society. In Hiro's view, "Asian parents don't explain things. It was a culture of learning by rote. Their children were going to schools where they were encouraged to ask questions, be analytical - so there was a clash."

Parker interspersed these voices with a stew of musical cues covering everything from 'Jerusalem' and the Troggs to Bollywood and Pakistani folk. Hiro remembers watching him sift through records in the World Service music library at Bush House: "He didn't understand the language but he understood the sound. His ear was impeccable. He could tell the real from the junk within a minute or two - he was an eccentric genius."

It's clear from audience feedback and press reviews at the time that this jumpy, impressionistic style was not for everyone. "The quick cuts and changes attracted attention to themselves and thereby detracted from the material" said one listener, while others were clearly exasperated that the subject was being given air-time in the first place. A BBC report concluded that some of those polled felt the blunter views expressed in the programme were "more likely to increase friction between the races". For Paul Ferris in The Observer Parker was "carrying technique too far", although Kathleen Rantell of The Glasgow Herald felt the programme had "tremendous

Charles Parker (Brian Shuel, 1965)

"In the past ten years, a third of a million Asian immigrants have transformed British attitudes from romance to fact. A real confrontation, and whether this results in understanding or prejudice - it's with us, on both sides. For the Asian teenagers, this confrontation with British society is itself a sort of unplanned political education..."

Extract from Stuart Hall's narration

"I think it's a good thing that negroes are rioting in America. It shows the country up, what it really is... if I was there, I would do what they're doing, make that country see that a man, a human being cannot be put down by a human being. I mean there's some people where I live, they call you black bastards and all that... What do you expect us to do, just sit there?"

– Jasbir Singh in Asian Teenager

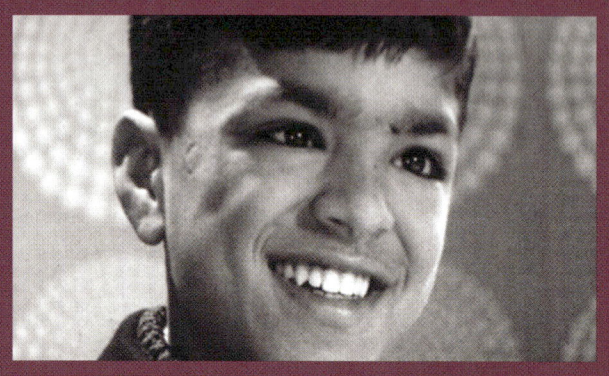

Mohammed Mossadeq (*Asian Teenagers*, 1968)

"Since all these people are beneficiaries of our Welfare State, having contributed nothing, it would have been more seemly if the BBC had not permitted the programme to include attacks on the Christian religion and the British Raj in India. Criticism is acceptable, but, in the circumstances, abuse is unpardonable."

– Housewife polled as part of BBC audience research following the first broadcast impact...nothing restores the human element more quickly and completely than a well-deployed tape recorder."

These broadcasts coincided with emergency parliamentary debates about Asian immigration from Kenya, and within a couple of months tensions were further heightened by Enoch Powell's speech at the Midland Hotel - a speech which crystallised many of the anxieties about white British identity implicit in the audience response to *Asian Teenager*. Dilip Hiro and another journalist John Heilpern were commissioned by The Observer to spend four weeks in Powell's home constituency of Wolverhampton, resulting in a centre-spread article on 'the town that has lost its reason', Hiro cataloguing the spike in racial attacks in the wake of the speech.

That summer plans were underway for a television version of *Asian Teenager* as part of the BBC's current affairs series Man Alive, once again drawing on Hiro's research. The selection of interviewees was further widened to include ebullient Bradford schoolboy Mohammed Mossadeq, and a besuited frontman added in the form of presenter Jim Douglas Henry. The contrast with the radio programme is most stark when one of the subjects, Satish and his colleague Warren, are followed on a works outing from the Black Country to Blackpool, where Henry trails them along the beach quizzing them about their friendship: "If it came to a fight between white boys and immigrants, would you fight on Satish's side?" Parker was not a fan, and in an outraged letter to producer Ivor Dunkerton he detailed his objections to the film's "Raj-like" perspective.

Hiro and Parker continued to collaborate throughout 1969 on radio documentaries about student protest and Black Power, and Hiro also worked with documentarist Philip Donnellan on an essay film called *Strangers in a Town* which weaves together Hell's Angels, Sikh bus-drivers and Polish shopkeepers to create a rather bleak tapestry of post-Powell Wolverhampton. In the meantime, Charles Parker managed a bewildering array of extracurricular activities. Along with campaigning, teaching and local folk music promotion he continued to work with the singers Ewan MacColl and Peggy Seeger as part of the Critics Group, in late 1969 producing a series of covert broadcasts on behalf of the Vietcong which were designed to encourage American GIs to defect. Parker may or may not have made use of his employers' facilities after hours to edit these programmes, but in any case he had become increasingly estranged from BBC management and was sacked in 1972.

All of Dilip Hiro's West Midlands experiences helped to inform his work on the script for *A Private Enterprise* (1974), the tale of a young, penniless Indian immigrant in Birmingham who makes an unsuccessful attempt to become a businessman by selling small, handcrafted elephants. The first feature film to explore the British Asian experience in any depth, its wry take on intercultural relationships and new age nonsense prefigures the work of Hanif Kureishi, although Hiro would become better known for his non-fiction writing on the Middle East and South Asia. When he returned to Birmingham for Flatpack's 2018 edition after many years away, he was not surprised to find the city once again completely unrecognisable.

WORK IS A FOUR LETTER WORD

"Welcome to Friday and another lovely day in your very own Domestic Industry Community Estate, in the throbbing heart of England." Propaganda chirps out of the radio as opening titles are stamped over a shiny new skyscraper. From a terraced street emerges a downtrodden array of citizens, heading for unspecified employment as exploited drones in the aforementioned skyscraper.

Work Is a Four Letter Word was the debut feature by theatre director Peter Hall, a product of that strange time when Hollywood studios threw money at unlikely projects in the hope that they would attract an elusive younger audience. The basis for the film was a stage play by Henry Livings called *Eh?* By the time it had reached the screen few traces of the original script remained, leaving instead a thoroughly muddled countercultural caper about mushrooms and mechanisation with a cast largely assembled by Hall from Royal Shakespeare Company regulars. David Warner is oddball Val, clad in a cellophane overcoat and determined to get a job in the D.I.C.E. headquarters so that he can cultivate hallucinogenic fungi in their boiler room. His fiancée Betty is played by Cilla Black, attempting to launch a film career and given very little to do apart from sing the theme tune and follow Warner around a semi-demolished Ladywood looking confused. Interviewed during a rain break on set by the Birmingham Planet, Black said plaintively: "if I ever have the chance of making another film, it'd be nicer in a warm climate."

In the course of our research I discovered that my neighbour Ellie was one of the extras in that opening sequence. Her friend's father was the live-in custodian at the building which served as the film's principal location. Auchinleck House was built in the early 60s and an anomaly among the decaying factories and back-to-backs which surrounded it - "as though it had landed from outer space." The girls had the run of the place, dancing around the empty floors and sunbathing on the roof. At some point they heard about the planned film shoot and managed to wangle themselves roles as extras. Ellie was already studying at drama school and taking part in theatre workshops at the Midlands Arts Centre, a place which she remembers as "somewhere you could become what you wanted to be, rather than what your parents expected you to be." She recognised many of the film's performers from bus trips to Stratford-on-Avon and was excited about a potential brush with movie glamour.

On the whole this did not really materialise, although she does remember sitting on David Warner's lap and talking to him about *Great Expectations*. The cast and crew were friendly, and the two friends were even allowed to attend private screenings of the film's rushes at the recently-completed Scala Cinema on Smallbrook Queensway. By the summer of 1968 when the film was released to audience indifference and critical derision, Ellie had moved on to London. She didn't see the completed film until it surfaced on YouTube a few years ago, and she was decidedly unimpressed. Peter Hall himself, stumbling across the film on television during the 1970s, recorded a similar reaction in his diary. "I made it in 1968 when I didn't know how to direct films and was anyway going through a very bad patch. Excuses? I suppose so. I watched with glazed horror."

Work Is a Four Letter Word may not have stood the test of time, but when we showed it on 35mm film as part of Flatpack's Birmingham 68 weekend the cinema was almost full. My guess is that most of the audience were there not to discover a forgotten classic, but to see a fifty-year old version of their own city. While the film may be a mess narratively speaking it does have some sharp cinematography by Gilbert Taylor, who plays up the visual contrast between crumbling Victoriana and sleek modernism to give a sense of the future-shock which Brummies were experiencing at that time. Auchinleck House is still standing, now in the form of a five star hotel, while Val and Betty's terrace is long gone and at the time of writing a luxury apartment block was springing up on the same site.

Work Is A Four Letter Word (Universal Pictures, 1967)

Ironic street sign (Nick Hedges, 1969)

GHOST STREETS OF BALSALL HEATH

After her Balsall Heath expeditions Janet Mendelsohn would often stop in for a cup of tea at Catherine Hall's house in Moseley. They talked mainly about their lives: "it was a friendship between two young women making their way in the world." Hall was expecting her first child at the end of 1968, and would eventually drop out of her PhD in medieval history to focus on parenting and the women's movement. Mendelsohn was from an affluent New York Jewish background, living in a strange city and becoming immersed in a world completely removed from her own. "She was like a foreign traveller - in that tradition of women travellers, ethnographic work and all of that - and she was able to be a participant observer in a way that would have been completely impossible for a British woman. I think she was skilled at it too. She created trust with the people she was photographing."

Balsall Heath was a magnet for journalists, photographers and social workers at the time, thanks to its high-profile notoriety as a red light district and multicultural halfway house. In contrast with the ground zero approach found in Ladywood, redevelopment was being deployed in a much more targeted way here. By 1968 a good deal of Varna Road had been demolished, less because of the poor quality of its large Victorian houses than because they were renowned for hosting a significant majority of the area's prostitutes. Although most of her photographs were taken a couple of blocks beyond the river Rea in the shops and cafes around Clevedon Road, Mendelsohn adopted Varna Road as the name for her project - an instantly familiar shorthand for the social ills of modern urban Britain.

The American may also have been aware of an article which had appeared in student newspaper Redbrick the previous year, featuring images of prostitutes on Varna Road taken with a telephoto lens from a passing car, and a report by an anonymous male student in which he describes sleeping with two sex workers. Mendelsohn's aim was to humanise lives that had become media caricatures of vice and poverty, and Hall believes that she was also motivated by "her incipient feminism, though she wouldn't have called it that at the time. She was interested in women's lives." Her final study would focus on one woman who became a close friend during this period of research, but the wider collection of negatives is less focussed on sex work than on the visual texture of the neighbourhood and the people who lived there.

These negatives formed the basis of an exhibition that we mounted in Balsall Heath itself during Flatpack 2018. Fifty years on, the pictures had taken on a completely different function. They documented streets that had been flattened and re-routed, terraces and alley-ways that had made way for grassy banks and maisonettes. One of the most popular elements of the show was a table given over to an enlarged Ordnance Survey map of the area. It was here that people would gather to pinpoint their old house or school, chatting across the generations while mentally reconstructing a childhood that had been swept away. A repeated refrain: "I didn't know we were so poor!" The cultural mix of the audience told its own story like growth rings on a tree trunk: the white working-class contingent of the 50s and early 60s; the mixed-heritage families of the 60s and 70s; and the more settled majority Asian population which has defined the area since.

Below: Janet Mendelsohn at Small Heath Fair, 1968

Opposite and following pages: Images of Balsall Heath (Janet Mendelsohn, 1968)

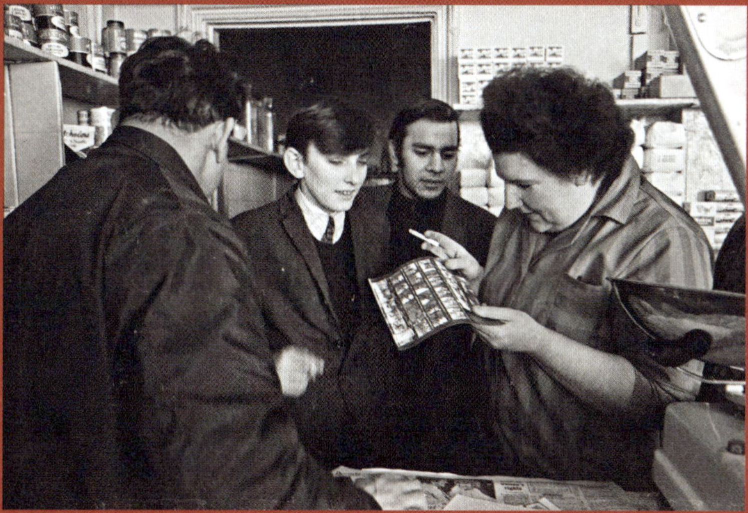

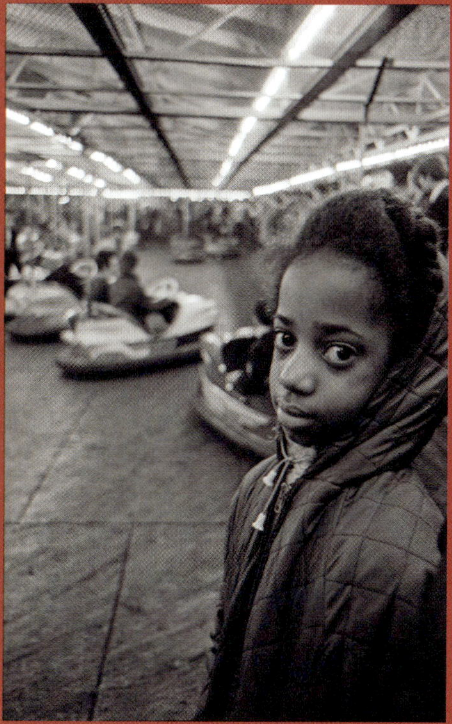

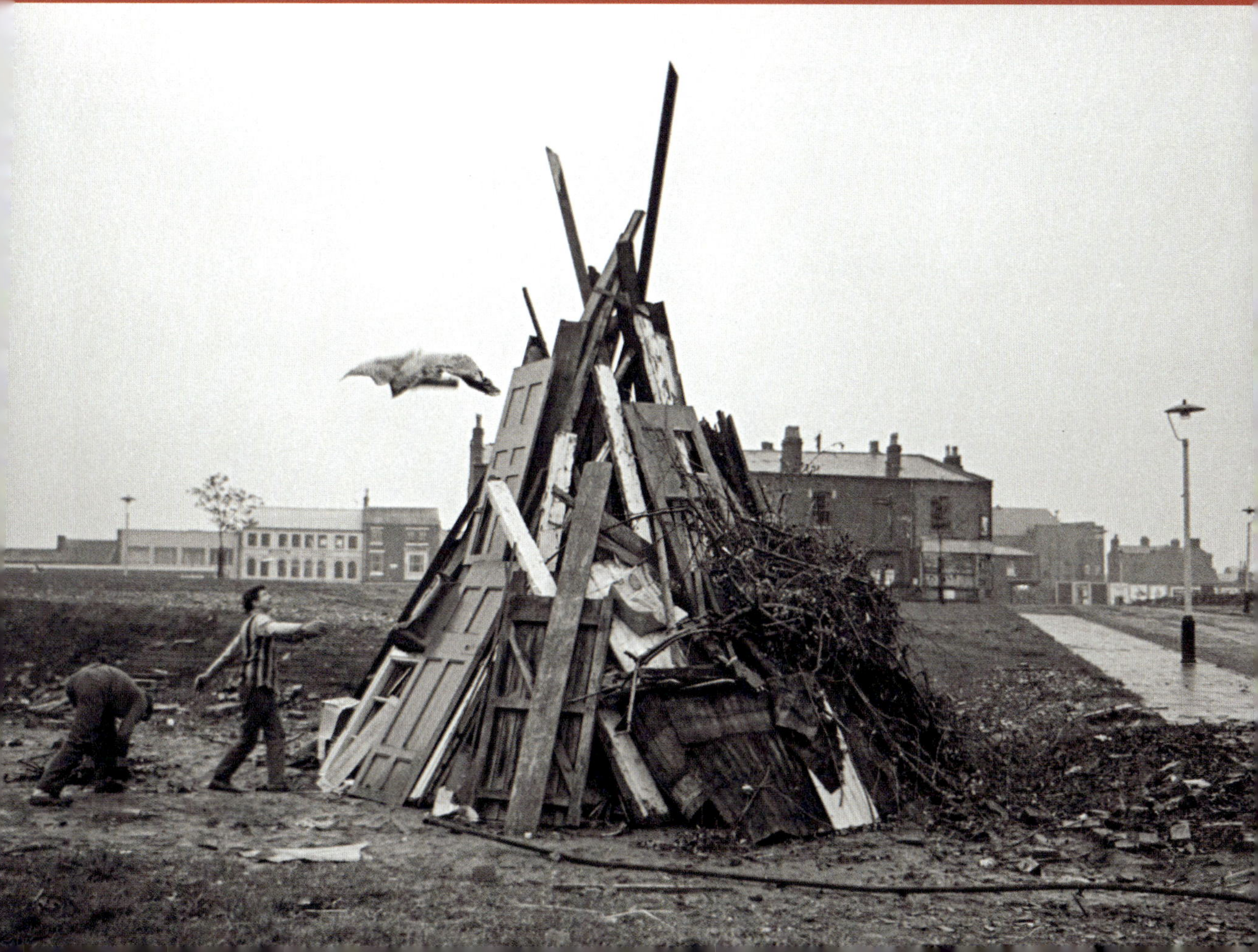

Tindal Street School

Lawrence Byrne (centre, looking left) remembers this photograph being taken. He lived directly opposite Tindal Street Primary School, and generally after the bell went he was out in the road having a kick-around. One day an American couple appeared with cameras. "I remember the accent... that's why we got excited, and inevitably we asked them 'Do you know John Wayne?' The cameras were massive. Nobody took your photograph in them days, apart from the police." The one holding the football is his older brother Kevin, aka 'Bullface', but it was Lawrence who could really play: "As soon as I got a ball I was in my element" For a shy lad these skills offered useful social capital - particularly after the school team's triumph over the all-conquering Moor Green team, whose pristine green kits were a sharp contrast with the Tindal St kids' vests and threadbare shorts. For sheer glory this would only be topped by an a capella performance of the Archies' 'Sugar Sugar' using cardboard guitars, which brought the house down at the end-of-year assembly.

Byrne was the second youngest of ten siblings, moved south from Lee Bank during redevelopment in the early sixties. The local cafés and bomb-sites provided as much education as school, a scene of improvised mayhem and a reliable source of revenue - whether it be Penny-for-the-Guy, carol-singing or 'scrumping and tatting'. Outside the neighbourhood the name of Balsall Heath carried some stigma, linked as it was with sleaze and scarcity, but like many others he recalls a sense of togetherness. "That picture epitomises what it was like then... we got on. There was no N-word. You didn't use racist terms if you fell out." Lawrence lost Kevin in 2014, and following a period of travel he has come full circle and works as a painter and decorator in Moseley. He first encountered the photo at the Ort exhibition and has since incorporated it into his business card, under the company name Angels With Dirty Faces.

Pyar ka Sagar Café, Clevedon Road

Kafait Shah now spends most of his time in his home city of Lahore, but for many years he made his living as a painter in Balsall Heath. This café mural was one of his first commissions.

"Art was my interest from a very young age. They weren't really teaching it in colleges, so I started to look around at the people who were painting cinema posters and so on. I went to one old master and said 'I want to learn this', and he said 'OK, come after school, and we'll see what you can do.' This was about 1961, and in two or three years I'd become a more mature painter and was helping out my teacher quite a lot.

I came to Birmingham in 1965. My father was working in a steel foundry in Blackheath, and he asked me to come and join him there. It was the middle of January, I spoke hardly any English, and I hated the work. We lived in a little house on Court Road. Any free time I had, I spent on my art, and through the factory someone took an interest and asked me to make a painting of Audrey Hepburn. After that I started to learn how the business worked in England and began to get little commissions from restaurants and cafés as well as for cinemas and advertising hoardings.

Balsall Heath was not in a good state at the time. For so long people had just been surviving. We had beautiful buildings like the Baths and the Art School, but a lot of the neighbourhood was just slums. When you live in a place for so many years it's hard to notice the changes, but then you look at old photographs and realise how different everything is now.

The murals in Pyar ka Sagar came about because the owner saw my Audrey Hepburn picture and said 'can you do something for me?' It was a lot of work, but the café became quite famous and people would come just to see the paintings. When you get a bit of a name in the community then it brings in more jobs, and although there have been some difficult periods I somehow managed to keep it going for all those years."

Uncle's, Highgate Road

Santokh Singh arrived in Birmingham in 1958, having trained as a metalsmith in the Punjab. He found work as a brake-fitter at Snow Hill Station, and also sold groceries door-to-door around Balsall Heath from a cart. Eventually he was able to open the shop above on Highgate Road and in the early 60s was joined by his three brothers (hence the name Uncle's). The woman pictured on the right is Mr Singh's wife Harbans Kaur, who passed away in 1977. Around that time the family moved their premises to Ladypool Road, where they continued in business until January 2018.

Shortly before Uncle's ceased trading after sixty years in business, we gave the family a handful of Janet Mendelsohn's photographs. It was Mr Singh's only record of his first shop, and one of very few images of his wife. He hung a framed print on the wall behind the till. A couple of months after Uncle's closed its doors for good, the *Ghost Streets* exhibition opened at Ort Gallery. Mr Singh attended the launch as a guest of honour and was repeatedly asked for selfies next to the photo of his original shop.

Traveller site, Sherbourne Road

The abundance of derelict land in Balsall Heath made it a popular spot for the travelling community, and from June 1968 a large camp took shape between Sherbourne Road and the new inner ring road. Percy Shurmer Junior School was right next to the site, pictured below in the background. Disgruntlement among residents grew throughout the summer and at the start of the new term a coachload of local parents presented a petition at the Council House demanding the travellers' removal.

On 12 September the Birmingham Post carried interviews with some of the travellers. "Fairly typical is Mr Jim Maloney. He was a labourer in Dublin. Most of his friends had crossed the Irish Sea in search of English streets paved with gold, so he decided to chance his arm. 'I have not always lived in a caravan, but if you are a foreigner in this country and have no particular trade to your fingertips what else is there?' ... A burly ginger-haired man said, 'We have been hounded around long enough. All we ask for is a permanent site in most areas. And we are prepared to pay £2 to £3 a week for these facilities. For years now we have been treated worse than dogs, and it is about time someone realised our need.'" Three days later the site was cleared by 60 bailiffs, 100 police officers and a convoy of Land Rovers and diggers. "As bulldozers moved onto the site to dig an 'anti-tinker' ditch around it, the chairman of Birmingham's Public Works Committee, Ald. Albert Shaw, said 'Thank God it's over... We shall continue to try and find a site for these people outside the city boundaries.'"

Producer Charles Parker had developed an interest in the subject while making his 1964 radio ballad *The Travelling People*, in which Birmingham's Labour council leader Harry Watton notoriously declared "one must exterminate the impossibles." In the wake of the Sherbourne Road clearance Parker helped form the West Midlands Gypsy Liaison Group to try and avoid similar situations in the future.

Cover of the Birmingham Post, 12 September 1968

00
LESS THAN NOTHING

"They seem to do such dreadful things... there seems such a cruel streak in them."

"I don't think they can think for themselves. They're just a pattern of ignorance."

"I feel terribly sorry for them - they're lost, they're lonely, and really they're awfully mixed up aren't they?"

Vox pops recorded outside Birmingham Cathedral by ATV,
for a 1968 report on the Double Zero

Birmingham's oldest district, Digbeth sits just south of the city centre. Dominated by the Bordesley Viaduct with various car-yards, nightclubs and creative businesses nestled under the arches below, you can also find the occasional manufacturing firm and corner pub bearing witness to the area's past as a buzzing industrial quarter. By the 1960s most of Digbeth's cramped, dilapidated back-to-back housing had been demolished, with a tiny residential population left behind and the local parish church looking increasingly isolated. In 1965 there was talk of closing down St Basil's for good, until an unlikely youth work project came along and transformed it into the focal point of the biker scene.

David Collyer had grown up on the south coast and learnt self-sufficiency from an early age. After leaving school at 16 he made a living as a bin-man and play-worker, before securing a place at Oxford and then going on to train as a vicar at Cambridge. During his time there he got involved in a community centre catering to local Teddy Boys and became interested in the growing field of work with 'the unattached' - young people who for whatever reason were not engaged with traditional youth clubs. Because his mother was unmarried, Collyer had to wait for special dispensation before being ordained ("I didn't quite belong, and I wasn't quite normal"), and then moved to Birmingham to take up his first post as deacon in the parish of Perry Beeches.

The Bishop of Birmingham at that time was Leonard Wilson, a survivor of torture in a Japanese prisoner-of-war camp and well known for his progressive outlook - he was an early supporter of women's ordination and reform of the homosexuality act. He created for Collyer the role of Chaplain for the Unattached, a form of "free-range clergy" that gave him the latitude to work with a range of youth subcultures across the city. After a fairly fruitless period hanging out with beatniks in Chamberlain Square ("too self-contained") and Mods in a range of bars and nightclubs ("too integrated"), the 'Swinging Vicar' began to explore the fringes of the city's growing Rocker scene - particularly outside the legendary Alex's Pie Stall, where you could find over a hundred motorbikes parked on a typical Saturday night. The majority of these bikes were still produced locally by the likes of BSA and Triumph, many of their riders working in factories and chafing against parental values forged by war.

Seen as grubby wasters, bringers of noise, fumes and aggro, there were very few places where the Rockers could gather apart from Alex's and a handful of biker cafés. Having gained some trust through terrifying induction rituals riding pillion at a hundred miles an hour, Collyer's conversation with the group quickly turned to the subject of finding somewhere to hang out. Bishop

> "I felt that I had to try and interpret what was going on... that what we were dealing with was the next generation of people, who were going to turn out to be alright."
>
> - Reverend David Collyer, 2018

Wilson (who would soon become known as 'Len the Bish') offered St Basil's as a stop-gap solution, and by the end of 1965 a delegation of leather boys was refitting the church as a biker coffee bar. This was not completely virgin territory for the Church - the Reverend Bill Shergold at the 59 Club in East London had opened a motorbike section in 1962 - but it was still a hefty gamble on Wilson's part. At one of the first meetings the group had to decide on a name and settled on the Double Zero ("because we're worth less than nothing").

As with the 59 Club, evangelism was not on the menu - Collyer's aim was to stay in the background, with the members dictating direction. "The first thing I said was: 'You appoint a chairman, you appoint a treasurer... You said you've never had anywhere to go, you said you've never had any chance of being involved in anything. You must take full responsibility for this if you want it.' And they did." A series of reports written for potential donors help to paint a picture of the club's growth, from the initial vanguard of 14 to 300 members by the time of the official opening in spring 1966, up to a thousand by the following February with a similar number of non-members stopping in each week. For Ray Fox, involved from the early days, it was "a safe haven - music, birds, noise, mucking about with your bikes, talking bikes, sleeping bikes." Barbara Haywood was a member and a regular coffee-bar volunteer who recalls a "vibrant atmosphere... in the '60s, for women to go on their own somewhere was a bigger issue than today, but I would go on my own knowing there would be people in there that I knew."

Visitors would find bikes filling the alleyway alongside the church and the small car park out back, while inside was the main cafe area lined with pinball machines and a jukebox, along with a workshop, a lounge area where somebody was generally crashed out asleep and a gym space for letting off steam. There was a fairly busy activity programme, but what members really valued about the DZ was the lack of structure and authority - the second report cheerfully states that "the club

"It was like being reborn. What's this world that's around me? It's hard to describe... It's like if you were living in a jungle and somebody blindfolded you and then brought you into the centre of Birmingham, in rush hour and cars and bikes and buses and thousands of people and shops and food and clothes and you didn't have nothing like that in the jungle, you'd think you were either dead and in heaven or what? It was a whole new world as far as I'm concerned and that's it."

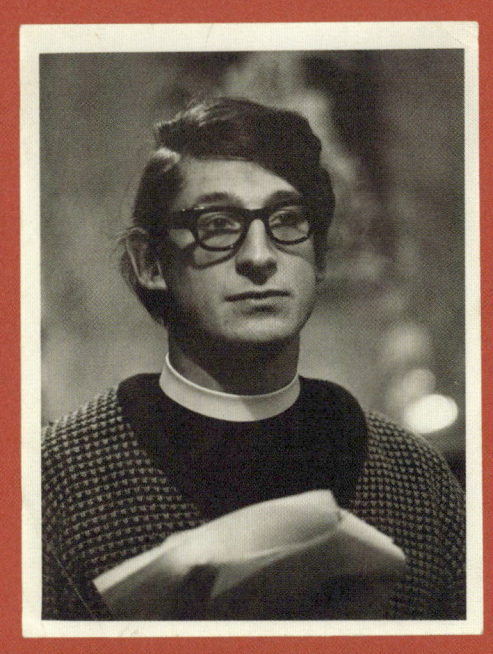

Top: Ray Fox and friend outside the DZ, c.1969
Bottom: Rev David Collyer, 1966

DON'T LET THIS LAD FOOL YOU —

INSIDE THIS JACKET IS A CITIZEN

'JOHN JOHN'

Detailed Programme 1/-

THIS WAY TO THE REVOLUTION

DOUBLE ZERO

DAVID COLLYER

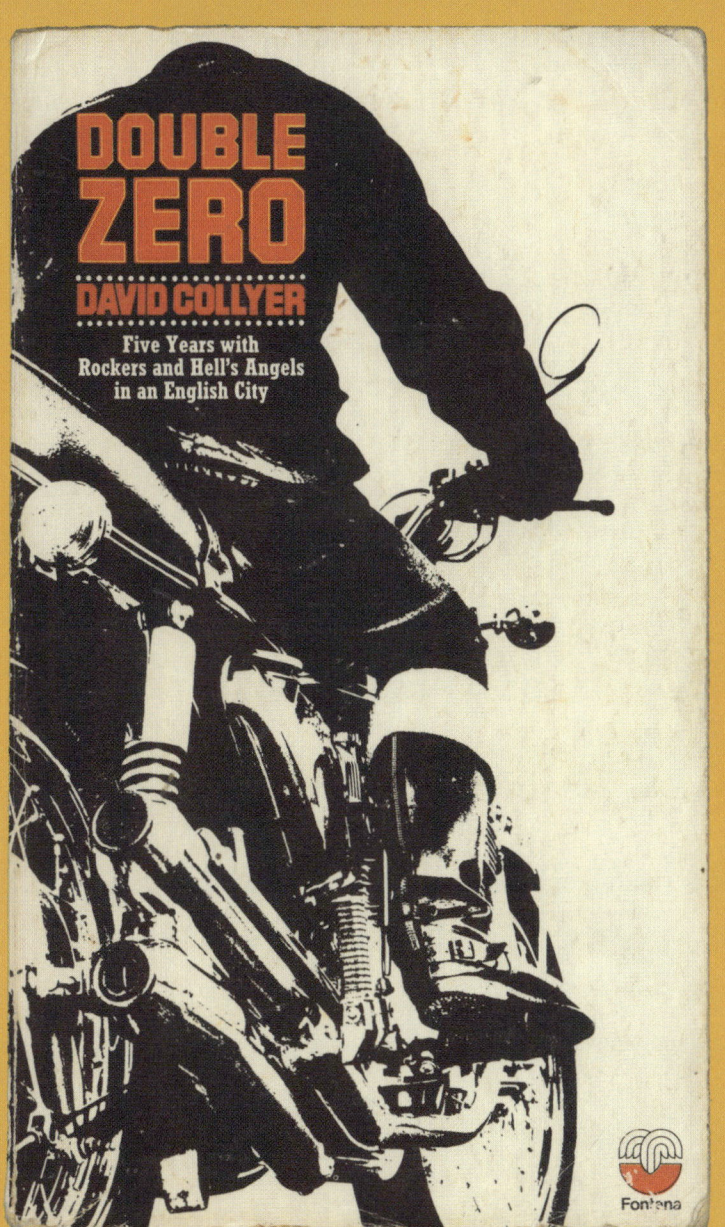

Five Years with Rockers and Hell's Angels in an English City

Left to right:

DZ fundraising leaflet, 1967

Double Zero by David Collyer (Fontana 1973)

DZ members jacket (David Rowan, 2018)

and the coffee bar have survived the first three months without a single rule." On the other hand it offered the sense of an anchor for young people with often turbulent lives, while growing up in a city that was changing on a daily basis. Collyer remembers: "The bulldozers were going through like crazy... It meant that people who lived back to back in communities were dispersed to Castle Vale and Chelmsley Wood where they weren't happy... People weren't ready for it and I think that's one of the genuine reasons that we did see a number of people back in Deritend - it was familiar stamping ground."

Part of the Double Zero's agenda was to connect members with the wider world in order to improve their public image and their employment prospects, through a range of schemes including sponsored walks, links with local businesses, civil defence volunteering and a dispatch rider service delivering blood and drugs to hospitals across the city. Some of this was rooted in the vicar's instinct for a good media gimmick: "Having been warned off publicity, I sought it." Describing the local press and television as his "first real support group", Collyer used eye-catching images - biker weddings, the juxtaposition of leather and dog-collar - to generate column inches and support his fundraising drive. He was also regularly paired with John English from the Midlands Arts Centre in media debates about the generation gap: "John was raising a fortune from places like the Arts Council, telling everybody that his was the most successful and best attended arts facility in the world and it was full of ordinary people. I was there saying all of this money is going to the elite."

There are frequent references to financial struggles in the DZ reports, and not just because they were written to solicit donations. In the summer of 1966 the bishop had to make a personal loan of £500 to keep the place afloat, and the following year a series of raids on the coffee-bar till led to a significant trading loss. Around this time the fundraising did begin to bear fruit though, allowing for a refurbishment of the main hall and expansion of the car park, while the stream of visitors to 'Dave's zoo' continued to grow. Much like the MAC, the Double Zero had become a case-study, an object of fascination for civic dignitaries, overseas youth-workers, media personalities and academics. One of the latter was Paul Willis, who arrived at the Centre for Contemporary Cultural Studies in the autumn of 1968 and was immediately electrified by the university occupation. His ethnographic work focussed on bikers and hippies and included research sessions where Double Zero members would play records and talk about their lives. The resulting PhD dissertation, which became the book *Profane Culture*, gives a darker picture of the scene than the official media narrative allows.

Death is a recurring theme in the conversations, and not just in the abstract - these young people were well used to losing friends in horrific accidents. In August 1967 alone the internal report records four member fatalities. "Practically every week you were going to a funeral" recalls Ray Fox, who felt that part of this death-wish was a hangover from the war: "There weren't no enemy apart from hitting the tarmac. It never appealed to me - if I was going to die, I wanted to die in bed with a cigarette in one hand and whatever in the other hand." Vietnam, assassinations, riots and the atomic threat also helped to fuel a broader darkness at work in the zeitgeist, spawning the likes of Black Sabbath and reflected in biker culture through the rise of the Hell's Angels. The Angels posed an existential threat to the Double Zero - violent, nihilistic, and unlikely to participate in five-a-side or sponsored walks. "I suppose it was a familiar situation," Collyer reflected shortly afterwards, "of a new generation turning up to destroy what the previous one had built."

Attempts to integrate them into the membership had mixed results, while other external pressures continued to mount. The club's relationship with the local police had generally been positive, and David Collyer was adept at schmoozing the City Recorder Michael Argyle in order to talk him out of his customary heavy sentences when DZ members took the stand. (Regularly distracted by the racing results in court, Argyle would become notorious a couple of years later as judge on the Oz obscenity trial.) However crime in Digbeth was on the rise,

> "I'd like to die racing down the road, down the bastard, give it almighty stick, give a jag a go, and then, you know, a fucking big lorry comes out, crunch, that's the end of you... nice, eh?"
>
> - 'Fred', interviewed by Paul Willis in 1969

a fact that was often pinned - fairly or not - on the Double Zero, particularly after one member was imprisoned for manslaughter. At one point the police threatened to close the place down. In the meantime, the climate was changing within the Church of England. Bishop Leonard Wilson retired in 1969, and although his successor expressed support for the project it was clear that patience for this more experimental, free-range approach was becoming limited. In Collyer's view, the Church became preoccupied with "preserving the institution and preserving what we had, rather than developing what might have been."

The vicar himself was burnt out from overwork, and despite growing a team around him there was no getting around the fact that the Double Zero was built in his charismatic, somewhat kamikaze image. In 1971 he took on the more strategic, city-wide role of Diocesan Youth Officer, and was replaced at St Basil's by the Reverend Les Milner who maintained business as usual for a short time but then quickly began to adopt a different tack. Having poured five years of himself into the place, missing out on a fair chunk of his childrens' development in the process, Collyer felt lost. An older mentor advised him to get his experiences down on paper, and the resulting three-week writing binge formed the basis of an occasionally schlocky but fascinating paperback published by Fontana in 1973.

Double Zero alumni may still quibble about some of the details in that book, but on one thing most of them agree: the club made a difference. For Barbara Haywood, its value was in "somebody saying, 'We've got these kids on the street... we need to give them somewhere to go and give them something in their lives to say that life is worthwhile.' When you've got that sense of purpose, you've possibly then got change." We spoke to many members who were helped out of a hole by DZ staff, whether it be through an honest conversation or a bed for the night. So many of the bikers had accommodation issues that at one point Collyer had considered the need for an emergency hostel, and in 1972 Les Milner converted the coffee-bar into an 18-bed dormitory for young men. The 'Boot Shelter' formed the basis of a youth homelessness charity which still operates today in the same building under the name of St Basil's.

David Collyer has since continued to work across Birmingham as a clergyman and fundraiser. When I approached him at home in Bournville he was wary of public appearances, having been charged in a civil case with embezzlement in relation to a Nechells regeneration project and subsequently declared bankrupt in 2013 (he continues to try and clear his name). He was more than willing to reflect on happier times though, and agreed to take part in an archive screening and conversation during Flatpack's Birmingham 68 weekend. Our choice of the MAC as venue caused some disgruntlement among DZ members - "why aren't you doing it in Digbeth?" - but thankfully a decent contingent turned out in the audience and contributed good-natured heckling from the back row throughout the discussion, just as they would have done fifty years previously. Ray Fox, the final committee chair and still a passionate biker, also took part in the Q&A. "It was like a cauldron of metal and oil and noise and being mixed up constantly for three or four years, until it was being stirred that fast that we were all shooting off in different directions and doing our own thing... Strange times, but good times."

THIS IS OUR LAB

LET'S NOT GET BUSTED

In September of 1968, Peter Stark began his first job as an assistant lecturer at Erdington Technical College. He had grown up in Newcastle and studied in Leeds, and came to Birmingham expecting to live with his girlfriend at the time. Unfortunately she fell in love with an Irish actor, so he found himself living in a flat in Gravelly Hill - where work was about to begin on the new Spaghetti Junction - and trying to find his way alone in an unfamiliar place. "It was a weird, weird time - this strange, modernist city centre that you could feel very lost in. I felt like I'd made a quite desperate mistake."

As for so many others, his first glimpse of an alternative Birmingham came through the underground press, thanks to the railwaymen who lived in the flat upstairs. "They used to get the International Times delivered, because the letters column of IT was one of the first places where the gay community was able to talk to each other." It was here that Stark heard about a series of music events under the name of Strange Days, raising money for a proposed Birmingham Arts Lab. He wrote to the organisers and received an encouraging reply from a Mark Williams, who it turned out had attended the same school as him in Newcastle.

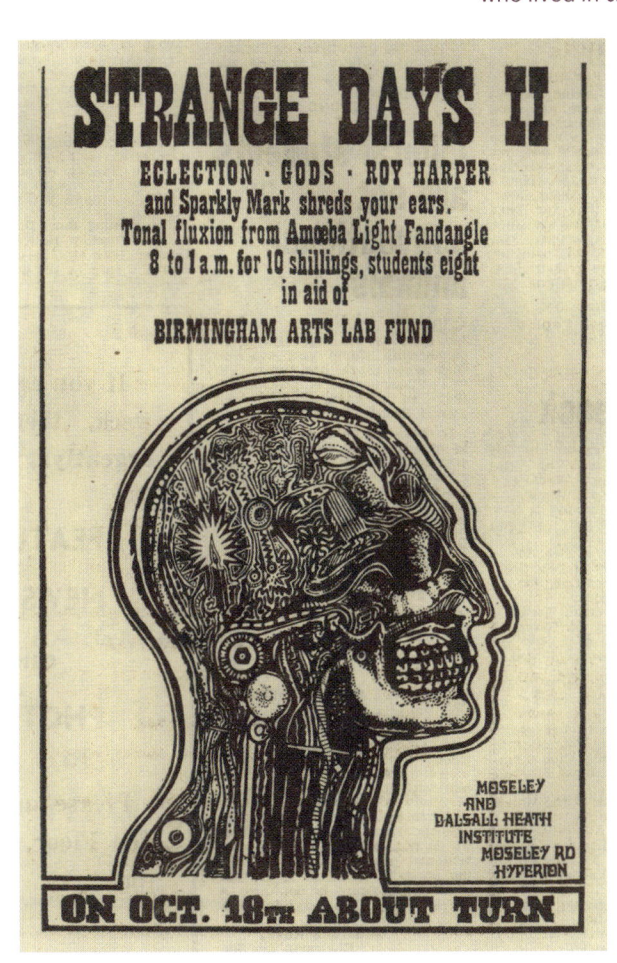

Williams had come down from the North East to work as an advertising copywriter and from late '67 became involved in the local music scene, DJ-ing at the legendary Shoop clubnight and organising regular music events at the Midlands Arts Centre (where Richard Rogers happened to photograph him - see p25). He was also distributing IT and Oz in the Birmingham area, picking up bundles of underground papers late at night from the station's Red Star depot, and through these networks he became aware of a burgeoning arts lab movement which was spreading across the UK.

The original model had been set up in summer 1967 by IT co-founder Jim Haynes in London's Drury Lane, and within a year or so there were close to 50 arts labs of different shapes and sizes around the country - including, briefly, one above a pub in Beckenham co-founded by David Bowie. The aim was to create a space for experimental culture across artforms, particularly in areas where more traditional venues were unlikely to venture - artists' film, progressive music, mixed media, performance art. Haynes spelt out four key principles: that a lab is an "energy centre" where anything can happen; it is non-institutional; the space can be used "in a loose, fluid, multi-purpose way"; and if possible it acts as a kind of commune, "where people can live and work together."

Advert for Strange Days II, 1968

Increasingly frustrated by the rules and restrictions at the Arts Centre, this was music to the ears of Williams and some of his fellow members. Their MAC events culminated in a free Roy Harper concert in the outdoor arena, but after John English refused to host another one for financial reasons the idea of an Arts Lab gathered pace. In late July the first event under the banner of Strange Days took place, with a light show and various bands including Spooky Tooth at the Carlton Ballroom in Erdington. After a public run-in with the Carlton owners (who Williams remembers as "local music business hustlers"), a second Strange Days event at the Moseley and Balsall Heath Institute was conceived as a fundraiser for a lab - or 'people palace' - and the publicity machine cranked into gear.

By this point Williams was an unofficial Midlands correspondent for IT, which certainly helped in getting the word out. He was frank about his frustrations with the "drag environment" in Birmingham: "the system has been run for too long by those who are in it for a fast buck, a big ego scene or because they have hopelessly misplaced their standards." Appearances on local TV and in the press helped to attract more punters to Strange Days II, and an article in Redbrick defined the Lab in opposition to its mothership - "like a garden to the arts centre's greenhouse" - while also giving some detail on the other members of the collective. Among them were Fred Smith, whose Amoeba Light Show was an important component of the live events, and self-described 'down-and-out technician' Tony Jones who was responsible for logistics and 16mm film screenings, and whose parents' home in Sparkhill had become a de facto HQ for the Lab-in-waiting.

After meeting the group at the Institute gig Stark became actively involved in helping them to find a building, and around the same time they were joined by art student Simon Chapman. He had a link with Peter Houghton at the Birmingham Settlement, who ran a youth centre north of the city centre in Newtown. On the first floor there was a disused gymnasium, and from early 1969 Chapman negotiated a series of pilot weekends to test out possibilities in the space. The first flyer included a map detailing their obscure location, and this offer: "if you want a coffee, good cheap food, a chance to talk, listen to interesting music, and watch experimental films... then you're very welcome."

Mark Williams had already left for London before these events took place, having been offered a full-time job at IT. He was also unhappy with the direction in which Lab plans were moving, and a series of letters between him and Stark from that period describe the painful process of translating utopian ideal into practical reality. Stark had written to IT with a progress report, implicitly targeted at his former comrade: "for sanity's sake let's stop kicking at each other - there's too much else to fight in this unreal hole." Williams responds by attacking the "shamateurism" and "adolescent business whims" of the Lab, clearly stung by the way things had ended in Birmingham. "When those in the alternative society openly, or perhaps not so openly, practise the ways of a society they reject, then things are getting bad."

During those early months the core group struggled to reconcile audience expectations with their own practice. By the summer they had cut down on public events and committed themselves to developing the space in earnest. Their plans are spelt out in a fundraising document called 'Building in Birmingham', which places the project in the context

Above: the original Arts Lab founders in Cannon Hill Park, 1968 - left to right: Mark Williams, Tony Jones, Bob Sheldon, Dave Cassidy and Fred Smith

Below: Peter Stark's Arts Lab membership card (Designed by Simon Chapman, 1968)

Opposite: Fundraising poster ('the high peering one' at Hyperion design, 1968)

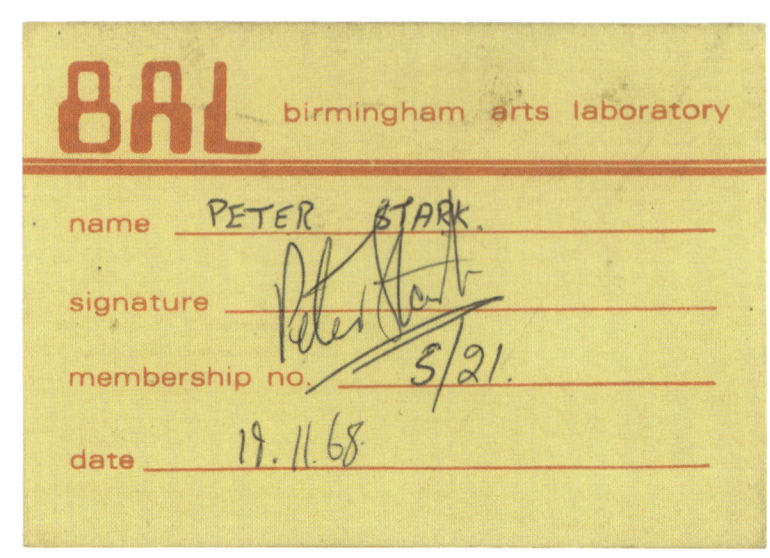

THIS WAY TO THE REVOLUTION

bal

birmingham arts laboratory fund
148, oakwood rd, birmingham, 11.
(021) 777 7034.

BIRMINGHAM ARTS LAB
NEEDS YOUR BREAD*
TO FEED YOUR HEAD

HELP prevent artistic famine in brum!
HELP open a people palace!
HELP!

support benefit events. donate to the fund. every little helps us and we are here to help you we <u>are</u> you. details from campaign headquarters.

*MONEY, CASH, LUCRE.

the high peering one

of the wholesale redevelopment going on around them, and early member Terry Grimley describes this period as "building an ark" in the face of the concrete tide. The document also contains an awkward mix of aspirations for an experimental arts space and slightly vague community aims, and on the whole it seems that the diverse and deprived Newtown population had limited dealings with the Arts Lab. As Stark puts it, "that community stuff drifted away."

The summer fundraising drive may not have been successful, but the Settlement continued to provide support in the form of extremely low rent. At the time Stark felt this was to enable the artistic work they were doing, but later realised that they were being subsidised as a "self-regulated youth group" - not unlike the Double Zero, although with oil-wheels and performance art instead of motorbikes and leather. The age range of the group was between 19 and 22, many of them surviving on the dole in order to commit themselves full-time to the project, and in the spirit of Drury Lane at least four members were living on the premises at any one time - in some cases sleeping in the mezzanine storage space between two floors. "We were like sardines", remembers Stark, "if you wanted to have a sex life you couldn't do it while being resident in the Lab."

Notwithstanding the lack of money or love action, this is a time fondly remembered by those involved. An auditorium was built up from nothing in the gymnasium, using borrowed projectors and scaffolding scavenged under cover of darkness from a nearby building site, later described by Lab regular and author Jim Crace as "the world's most uncomfortable cinema." An ad hoc family structure emerged, fuelled by murky coffee, beer from the pub across the road and the occasional spliff - although given that this incongruous new venture attracted some interest from the local constabulary, members had to be fairly cautious about drug use. "This Is Our Lab," read a sign at the top of the stairs, "Let's Not Get Busted."

A public programme had been maintained through various gigs including the Free Balsall Heath Festival, where the Lab team put on local bands like Bachdenkel and Earth - recently renamed as Black Sabbath. (Stark recalls the latter using the Lab to rehearse their new single 'Paranoid' repeatedly for a fortnight, leading to complaints from the landlord about the "dreadful cacophony of noise"). By the autumn they were ready to let general audiences back into the Tower Street space, and Bryan Brown in the Lab's burgeoning print workshop began to churn out brightly coloured promo posters. These would be pasted up in underpasses and back-streets during night time raids on the city centre, using a specially modified fly-posting overcoat with false arms.

By this point film had become an important part of the Lab programme - partly because it was less expensive to mount than theatre or gigs, and also because a cinephile core had formed within the group with Tony Jones joined by Anil Bhalla and Peter Walsh. Among the

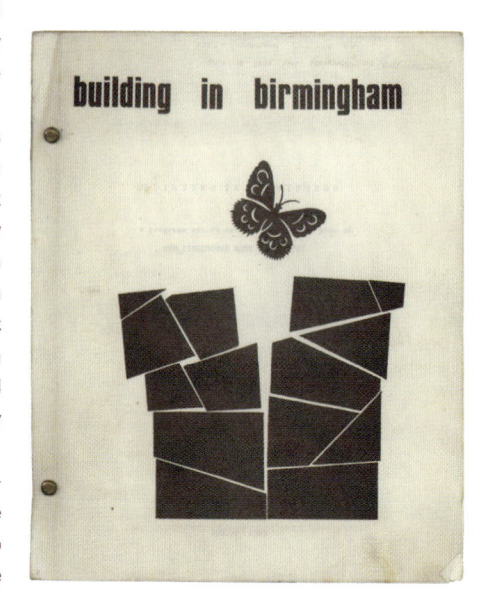

> "The current spate of building in Birmingham has completely changed the face of our city. Physically, Birmingham is the city that belongs most characteristically to the twentieth century. It is bright, new, glossy and functional. But is this enough for those who live in it? Beautiful or new buildings do not necessarily enable people to live happily with each other and other groups."
>
> Building in Birmingham, August 1969

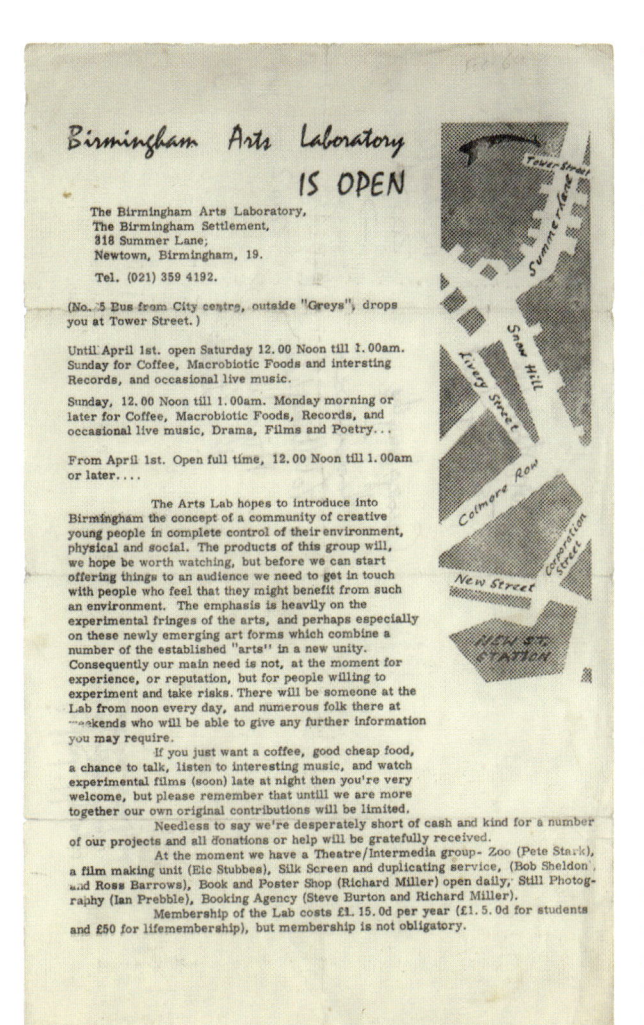

attractions in that autumn programme are Buñuel's *The Exterminating Angel* and Godard's *Weekend*, the sort of titles which would be unlikely to get an outing in Birmingham otherwise and which drew a curious new audience into Newtown. Beyond film the line-up includes experimental theatre stalwarts like The People Show and Welfare State, 'a multi-media jam session from Leicester' and an evening of West Indian performance devised by Balsall Heath-based Jamaican expat Hope Howard.

The schedule also features a discussion event titled 'What To Do With £1700', a regional meeting of the Arts Council's New Activities Committee. This initiative had been established earlier in 1969 following pressure from some of those involved in the lab movement, who felt that the Arts Council was unresponsive to cross-media work or activity taking place outside of traditional performance venues. Peter Stark became the committee's Midlands coordinator, responsible for allocating said £1700, and at the meeting it was agreed that the bulk of it would be spent on developing the Birmingham Arts Lab's space and programme. This was the first public funding which the place had received, a welcome shot in the arm at a time when many other labs were beginning to fizzle out due to lack of resources or energy.

A personal donation from Michael Astor, chair of the committee, had already enabled the Lab team to invest in a range of kit. Stark - in his role as "the responsible hippy" - bought a new IBM electric typewriter for creating elegant fundraising letters. "I used to wear frayed jeans and a smart blazer and make sure that I had the Third Programme playing quietly in the background when I took phone calls." Subsidy also meant scrutiny. In March 1970 the Daily Mail ran a piece headed "How YOUR cash is being used to finance hippy 'art.'" It was generally outraged about the New Activities Committee, and particular attention is given to Stark, described as "a director (unpaid) of Birmingham Arts Laboratory, which is housed in a ramshackle building in New Town, Birmingham. His weekly £6 Arts Council grant is his only income." It continues: "Activities in the Arts Lab include electronic music and light shows. Girl members often paint their faces and bodies and simply sit around."

Eagle-eyed readers will note that this is the first mention of female Lab members. Fully clothed and non-painted women played a role both behind the scenes and onstage, particularly as the 1970s progressed, but at this stage it's fair to say that the place was male-dominated. On the other hand these blokes were keen to distance themselves from prevailing modes of West Midlands masculinity, described by Mark Williams at the time as "a local patriotism based on beer and short-haired manliness." Epitomised by the iconic 'Ansells Bittermen' of a long-running advertising campaign, this culture would be parodied by poster artist Bob Linney in one of his Lab recruitment posters.

Throughout 1970 Birmingham Arts Lab made the tricky transition from non-institution to institution, balancing the books with a

Opposite and above:
Arts Lab fundraising brochure and launch flyer, 1969

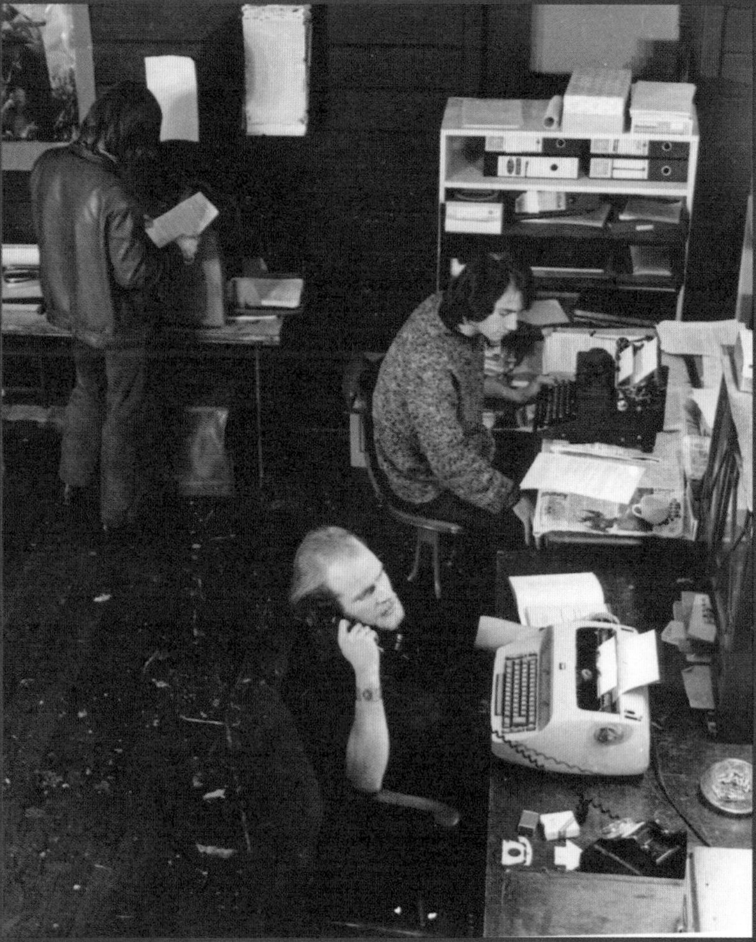

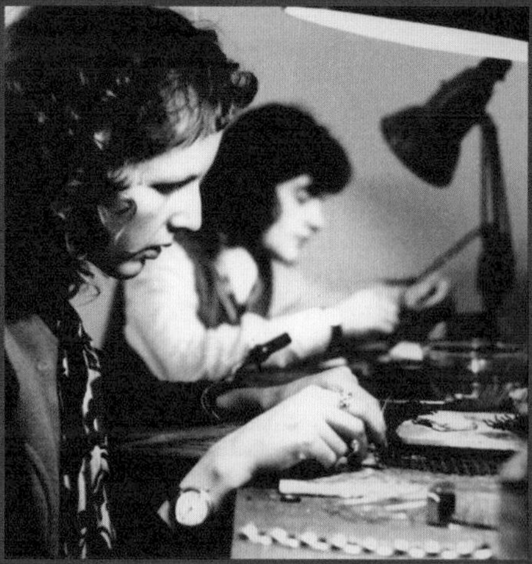

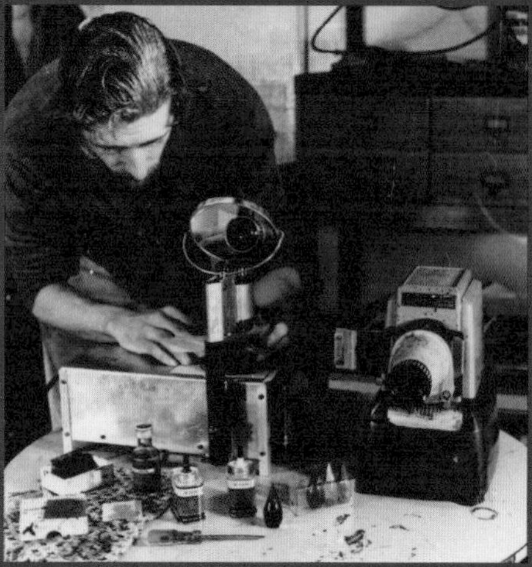

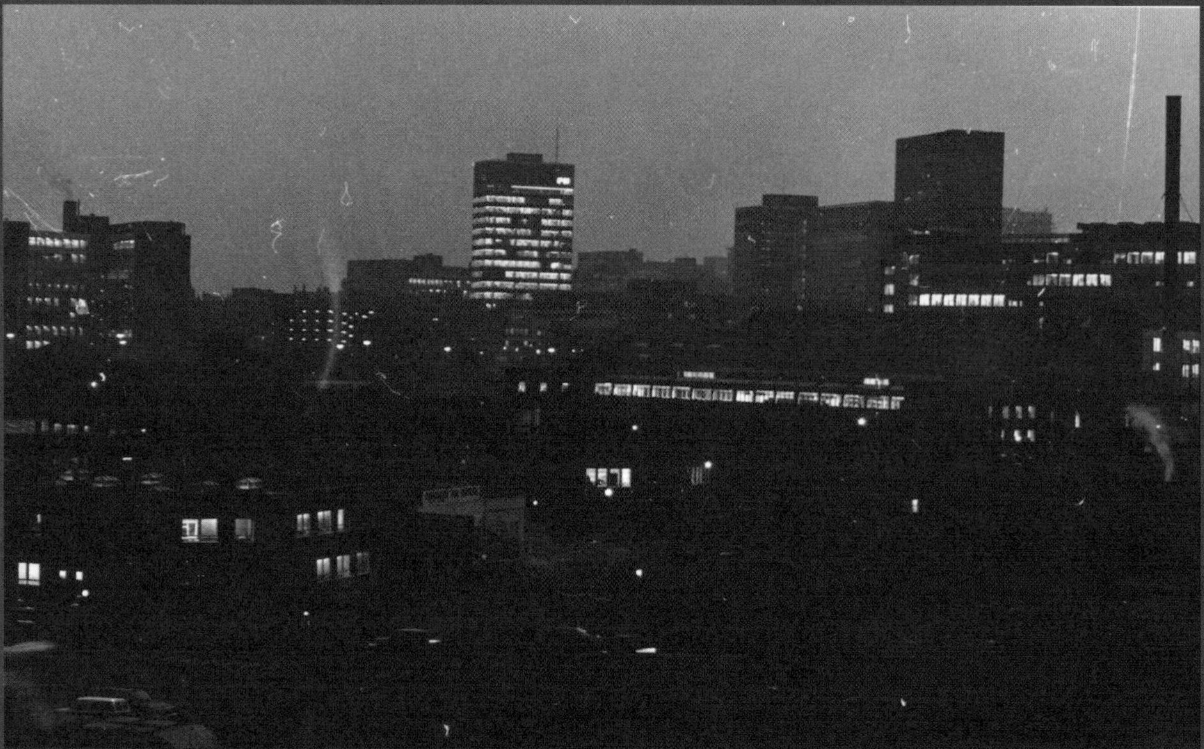

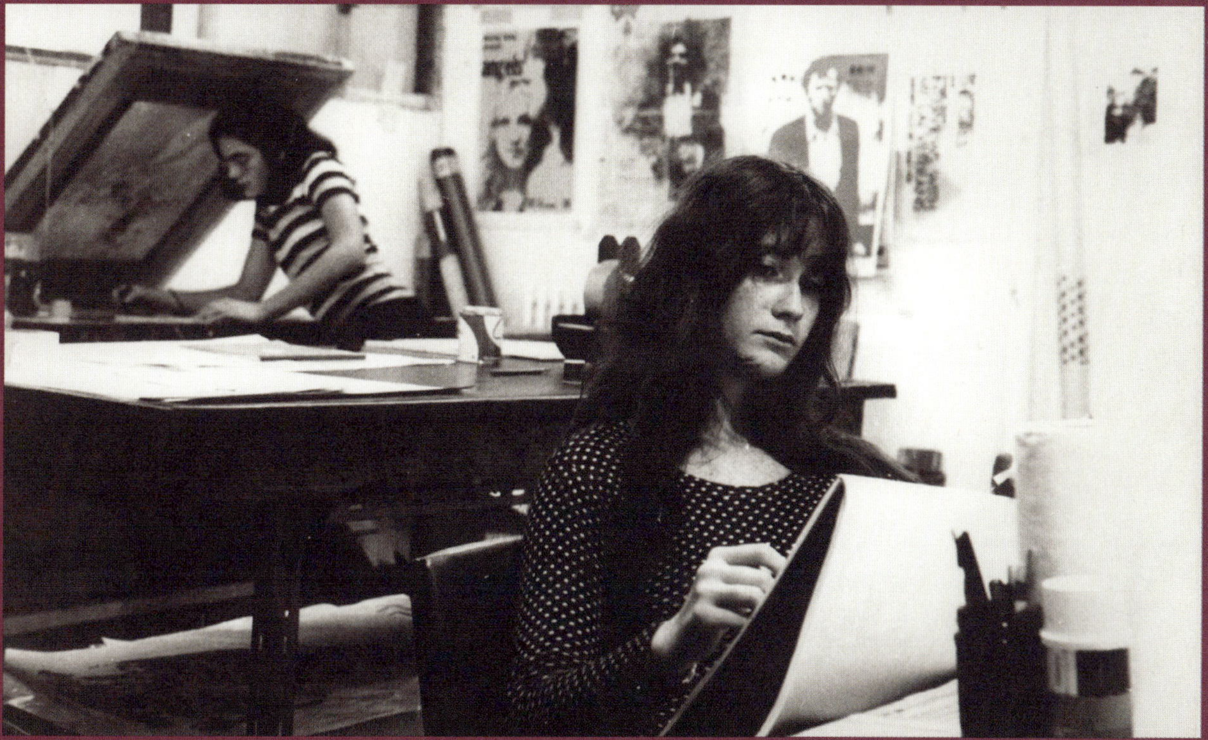

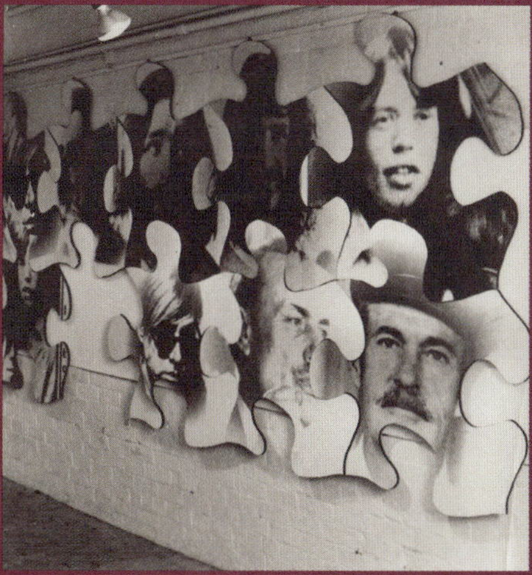

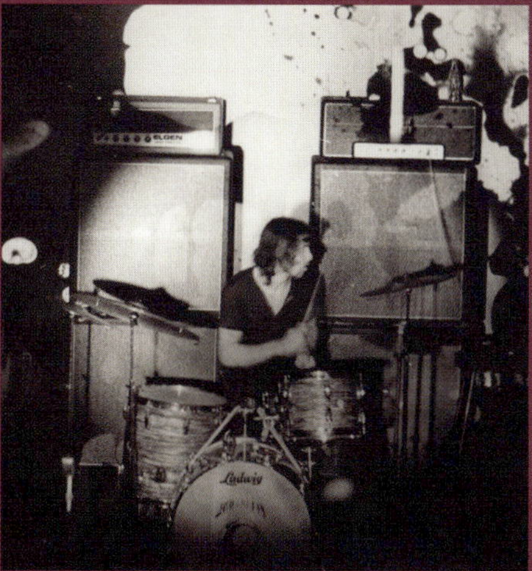

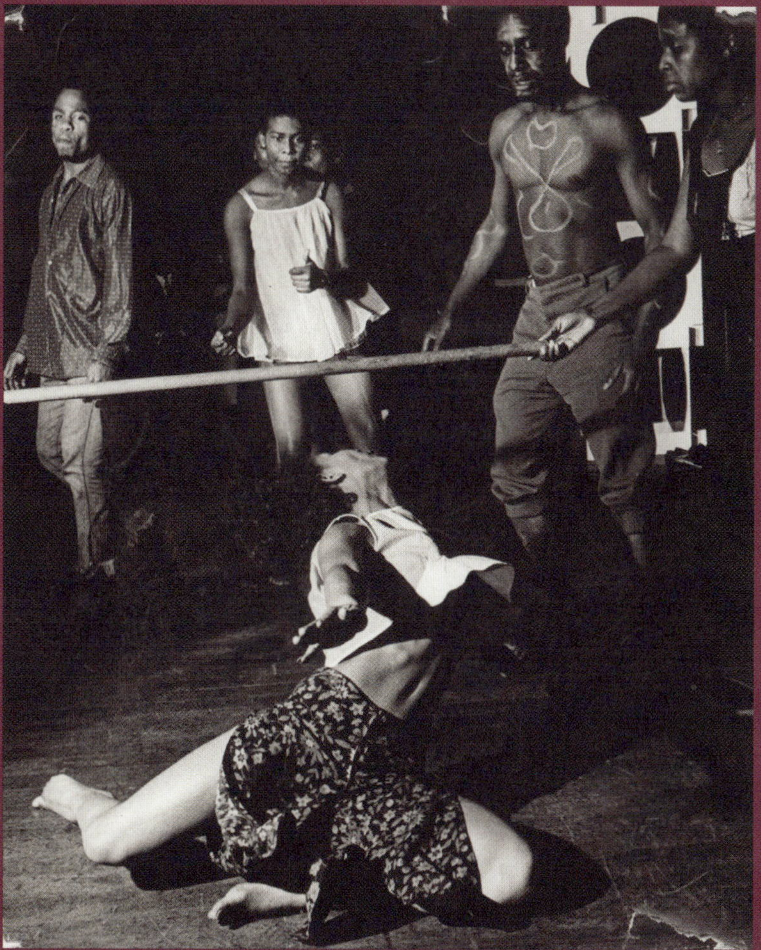

combination of cinema box office, coffee bar income and public funding. By the end of the year things were in a healthy place with a varied programme and over 1,600 members, but some of the original instigators were exhausted. Peter Stark had begun to look elsewhere, keen to reconnect with community theatre and his native North East, and together with Simon Chapman he drafted an SOS letter to the membership. "It seems foolish to contemplate closing the project when so much has been achieved but the people running it have run out of enthusiasm and energy and one of the key members is leaving. Can you help?"

Chapman assumed Stark's fundraising and admin role for a period before going on to run Ikon Gallery, and then Irish administrator Ted Little took the Lab to a new level of ambition: an influential print workshop led by Bob Linney and Ken Meharg; a city-straddling performance art festival; a varied experimental music programme; and a comics press featuring work by Steve Bell and Hunt Emerson as well as Suzy Varty's pioneering feminist comic Heröine. Long after the other labs had folded, Tower Street continued to flourish and provide a reliable launchpad for arts careers and for new work. Tony Jones would go on to establish the national Picturehouse chain, while Stuart Rogers, who as a 21 year-old in the early 70s was given control of the Lab's theatre programme, would return to the city many years later as Chief Executive of the Birmingham Rep. In 1977 the old youth centre on Tower Street was finally vacated for shiny new premises on Holt Street, with Aston University as unlikely landlords. This arrangement never entirely worked and by 1982 the organisation had morphed into the Triangle Cinema, still programmed by Pete Walsh and showing a wide range of international film but lacking the stew of different artforms which had made the original Lab unique.

The story of Birmingham Arts Lab could make a whole book in itself. A useful basis would be the catalogue produced by Birmingham Museum & Art Gallery in 1998, supporting a 30th anniversary exhibition of posters and ephemera. Terry Grimley, who after leaving the Lab became arts editor of the Birmingham Post, wrote the main elegy: "The Arts Lab provided Birmingham with a window on what was new and innovative in the arts for a decade and a half, as well as being a rallying point for young talent, eccentrics and free spirits growing up in the city or passing through its various educational establishments. In this way, it filled a role in the city's cultural life which has never really been replaced."

Many arts organisations working in Birmingham today still cite the Lab as a touchstone - not only for the eclecticism of their programming, but also their pragmatic approach to working with the materials and spaces available to them at the time. After helping to build the place up from scratch and remaining involved at board level following his departure in early 1971, Peter Stark still glows when describing the frontier spirit which animated the Lab's early years - "that sense that we could do things in these rooms, that we had the freedom to be ourselves, to make our own future."

Previous page:
Images of Birmingham Arts Lab by Simon Chapman, 1969-1971.

Left hand page:
The Arts Lab office, with (from top to bottom) Tony Jones, Terry Grimley and Peter Stark;
Jewellery workshop;
Alan Wilkinson, light show artist;
The city skyline from the roof of Tower Street, including the recently completed Post & Mail Building in the centre.

Right hand page:
Laura Mulligan in the print workshop;
This Could Happen To You, installation by Simon Chapman;
Unknown group performing with Amoeba Light Show;
Hope Howard's West Indian Dance Group.

Below: Lab membership poster (Bob Linney, 1973)

Opposite: Mike Westbrook Brass Band with Newtown kids (Tony Jones, c.1970)

THIS IS OUR LAB – LET'S NOT GET BUSTED

MOTHERS DAYS

BY EDWARD JACKSON

THIS MEMBERSHIP CARD
IS ISSUED FOR THE
SOLE PERSONAL USE
OF THE REGISTERED
HOLDER

*MOTHERS HIGH ST.
ERDINGTON TEL. 373 5514

MOTHERS
DISCOTHEQUE & TOP GROUPS

Furniture outlets, gentleman's tailors, and rock venues do not normally occupy the same building, but from 1968 to 1971 an unassuming, box-like structure on Erdington High Street contained all three. If by day you could visit the ground floor to buy a dinner table from Dale Forty, or a waistcoat from Brooks Bros., by night, one storey up, you could see the likes of Pink Floyd, Fleetwood Mac or The Who. The retail space exists today as a supermarket, and it is easy to miss the blue plaque that was unveiled in 2013 to commemorate the club that existed above. Ask anyone who went there, though, and you will hear the same response – Mothers, as it was then known, was the best music venue in the world. This isn't hyperbole; Billboard Magazine gave it that very accolade in both 1969 and 1970. But how did a small building in Erdington become a haven for progressive rock music?

"We were promoters in the true sense of the word," says founder John Taylor. "We promoted music right across the board." That 'we' included him, Phil Myatt, Gary Surman and John Singer, and as Taylor remembers, "we started just in the back room of a pub playing disco music – that was the early 60s." Mothers' true mother, as it were, was The Carlton Ballroom, which this entrepreneurial foursome began renting out on Saturday nights as they extended their operations. Soon enough, they were making so much door money they could buy the place, whilst also putting on discos in several pubs across the West Midlands. It's a reflection of the get-up-and-go spirit of the time that none of the men had started out in the music business; Myatt, for one, was a merchant seaman, and Taylor worked at an opticians.

This DIY ethos also informed the design of Mothers. Faced with blacked-out rafters, Taylor used skylights and string to create the illusion of a ceiling. He also built speaker cabinets himself, and hired light show projectors "from the local photo store. I used to pick them up on a Saturday and pay them the rent until Monday." The name change is attributable to Myatt, who claims he plucked 'Mothers' from a film starring Paul Newman and Ronald Reagan - an offbeat origin only undermined by the fact that the two men never appeared on screen together. A likelier story is that Myatt cribbed the name from The Mothers of Invention, piggybacking on the band's underground cachet so as to appeal to audiences hungry for more experimental fare.

It's much easier to say when Mothers officially opened, as in his booking diary from the time, Taylor circled 31 March 1968 and wrote 'Opening as "Mothers"' next to it. Even so, birth pangs would persist well into the summer, as the word 'Carlton' continued to appear on different days to 'Mothers' throughout June and July. Mothers emerged incrementally, sharing the same space as the Carlton Ballroom before eventually supplanting it. Like all shrewd businessmen, Taylor and his colleagues tested the waters before drinking the Kool Aid, waiting to see if psychedelia would be lucrative enough to invest in. They'd made up their minds by the end of '68 – as drummer Robert Moore relates, by then the club had evolved "from a dance club into an underground club - they made it really dark and dingy," put up "psychedelic lights and posters, and altered the stage."

These changes couldn't dispel a certain grottiness, though, for as Graham Holyoak recalls, "it was the scruffiest place on earth – dirty floorboards, usually slipping on spilt beer. The toilets - you really don't want to know about the toilets. But it was just...you got to go." As *the* place to be, Mothers' popularity often exceeded its capacity – officially licensed to hold 350 people, one New Year's Eve event held around 1,000. "It was always packed," fellow attendee June Nichols remembers, and with queues to get in regularly leading all the way down Erdington High Street, admission was by no means guaranteed.

This is despite the fact that Mothers was a members-only enterprise. As Kevin Duffy notes, "for 2s. 6d you could sign up and receive one of the hallowed orange and purple membership cards," and around 45,000 people did so. Who, then, was paying 2 shillings 6 pence (about £2.20 in today's money) to walk up a rickety stairway into a dim, squashed room? David Darkes recalls 'an awful lot of denim, and boots, long hair... It was very much a studenty kind of vibe'. That said, visitors came from all over the world to experience 'the home of good sounds' – rumour has it that Bob Dylan and Joan Baez were members (though they never played there). Comparable only to London's Marquee Club for the range and status of its acts, some of whom were joined by John Peel as a guest DJ, Mothers was well on its way to becoming a legendary establishment.

Not everyone was happy with this. Already frustrated by the obstacles he faced in setting up the Arts Lab, Mark Williams wrote to International Times in 1968 to lambast those he believed were exploiting the scene "for a fast buck." For him, this included the organisers of Mothers. Having been offered "a regular weekly venue there" for "a multi-media event called Strange Days", he accused Taylor and company of not only quickly withdrawing their support, but of stealing his idea. Taylor spat back in the following issue: to the charge they had "cashed in on the scene," he retorted that "this seems to be all in his mind as we had already had at the club (before Mr Williams showed his face) such groups as Spooky Tooth, Chicken Shack, Fleetwood Mac, John Mayall, Fairport Convention, Jethro Tull..."

Those inside Mothers were perhaps oblivious to such acrimony (although copies of IT, as well as the more hippie outré Gandalf's Garden, were on sale at the club). In ex-member John Chadney's recollection, "I can't remember there ever being any trouble. Everybody just accepted each other." However, for those whose job it was to keep order, the mood was rather different. Philip Took, a bouncer at Mothers, is sure that "if I went down the high street next Saturday, I would bump into somebody who would know me. They'd say, 'Hey, you used to work at Mothers Club!' I'd say, 'Yeah, did I smack you?' And they'd say, 'Yeah, and I smacked you!'" Far from hand-holding, Took recalls getting into fights, searching for concealed house bricks, and trying to brush off inquisitive policemen.

A carnivalesque spirit also made itself known at some of the performances. Taylor, for one, recalls "crawling around the floor with Keith Moon on my back, absolutely stoned out of our brains." Cannabis was profuse – "you couldn't escape it, basically," says the leader of Birmingham group The Idle Race, Dave Pritchard – but the management were willing to turn a blind eye, so long as things stayed mellow. This general informality between punters, performers and promoters is a key reason why Mothers lodged itself firmly in the hearts of its attendees. It is difficult to imagine a situation nowadays in which, as The Idle Race bassist Greg Masters reminisces, "you'd be at the bar and you'd turn around and there would be Rod Stewart, drinking."

Today this calibre of star can fill stadiums, or take up residencies in Las Vegas casinos – indeed, Elton John played at Mothers the night before it closed for good. Taylor blames the performers for the club's demise – "they just got greedier and greedier and greedier," as he puts it. But individual avarice only partly accounts for Mothers' end. As the 1970s dawned, universities – better funded and with bigger spaces – began to hoover up the acts. As John Singer told Laurie Hornsby, for the latter's 2003 book *Brum Rocked On!*, "in total innocence, we at Mothers had helped to create a market place that the club could no longer compete in." As with Bill Graham's Fillmore East and West across the pond, Mothers shone brightly and then quietly disappeared, a casualty of its own success.

Approximately half a century since its heyday, though, it still crops up in the news. In a 2016 court case, Los Angeles band Spirit alleged that it was whilst watching them play at the club on 31 January 1970 that Robert Plant nicked the riff for 'Stairway to Heaven' from their song 'Taurus'. "I really don't recall any of the bands I saw there or everyone I ever hung out with," said Plant in his defence. He must be unique, because Mothers left an indelible mark on everybody else. Though in many respects an ad hoc response to short-lived musical trends, the legacy of Mothers will long outlive the sterile hangars that house today's rock concerts – an unrepeatable combination of right place, right time, and good sounds.

Text by Edward Jackson. The interview with John Taylor was conducted by Jez Collins for the Birmingham Music Archive in 2018. Sarah Wilson gathered the Mothers reminiscences as part of a 2014 project for Birmingham Town Hall, with additional interviews by Birmingham 68 volunteers Joe Georgiou and Rebecca Took.

MOTHERS FACTS

Pink Floyd's 1968 record *Ummagumma* was partly recorded live at Mothers. Canned Heat also namecheck the club in the sleeve notes of their 1969 compilation album *Canned Heat Cook Book*, whilst The Who played their rock opera *Tommy* there two weeks before its official London debut.

On 12 May 1969, a van carrying Fairport Convention back from a gig at Mothers veered off the M1. The band's drummer Martin Lamble and Jeannie Franklyn, the girlfriend of guitarist Richard Thompson, were both killed.

It was whilst playing keyboards with Chicken Shack at Mothers that Christine Perfect became friendly with future husband - and fellow Fleetwood Mac bandmate - John McVie.

The club hosted its fair share of local bands, including The Moody Blues, Trapeze, Raymond Froggatt, Band of Joy and Black Sabbath.

Mothers didn't just provide cool music, but hot food as well - according to legend, it was the first place in Birmingham to have a microwave oven.

John Peel was a regular guest DJ and shared some of his memories of the place with Kevin Duffy in 1997. "I sometimes get mail from younger people who live in Birmingham and are amazed to hear that for a few years, the best club in Britain - and it was, because I went to most of them - was right there in Erdington."

Mothers membership card and ephemera courtesy of Syd Wall

Opposite: Mothers audience member (Birmingham Evening Mail, c.1968)

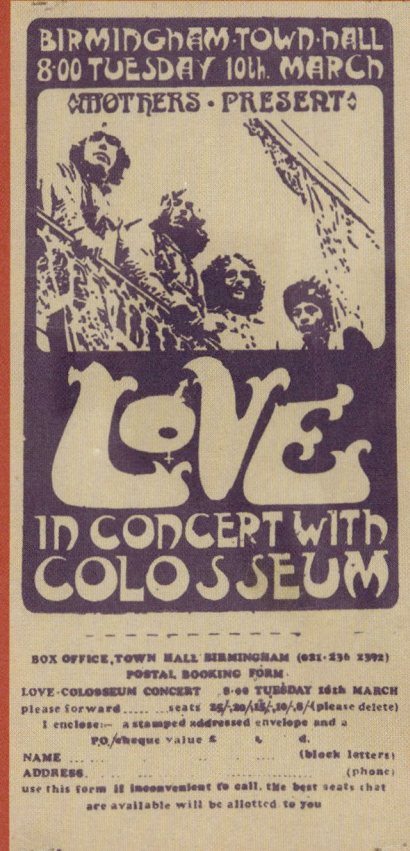

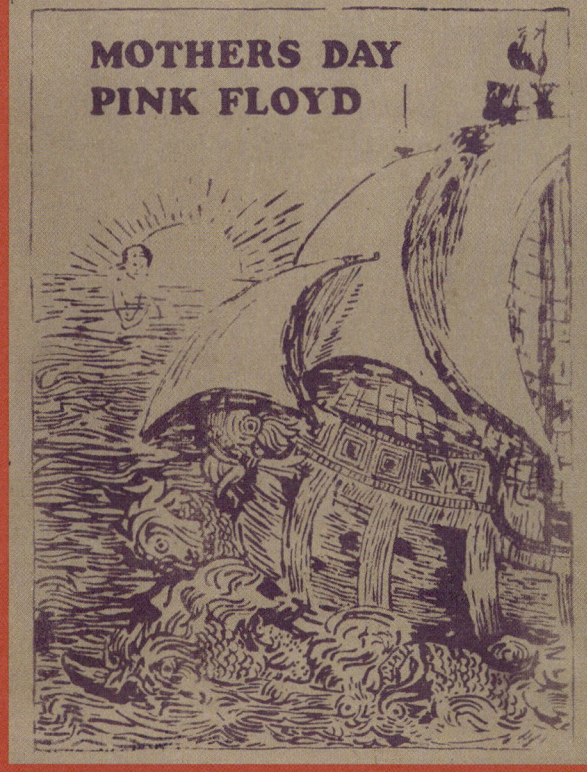

MOTHERS DAYS

While Mothers was making its transition from occasional gigs to fully fledged mecca for heavy heads, another regular event had sprung up to act as a beacon for the city's progressive music scene. From June 1968 Henry's Blueshouse took over the room above The Crown pub on Station Street every Tuesday night, with long-haired local support acts warming up for an impressive range of visiting blues legends including Arthur 'Big Boy' Crudup, Homesick James and Champion Jack Dupree. An appreciative audience sat cross-legged on the floor, while 16mm Laurel and Hardy films played in the side room. Set up in tandem with a new management stable called Big Bear, the night would become an important launchpad for emerging bands - including one noisy four-piece that would go on to achieve global fame.

Rev Gary Davis at Henry's Blueshouse, with Jim Simpson sat on the right (Norman Hood, 1971)

THE
BIG BEAR
FFOLLY

Jim Simpson started Henry's in order to put on a gig by one of his favourite local acts, Bakerloo. A jazz nut who grew up in the Black Country, his love of music was first given free rein while stationed with the air force in Gilbraltar during the 1950s. After a blissful period playing trumpet in honkytonks for sailors on shore leave, he settled back in the Midlands in 1962, taking photographs for Melody Maker and Midland Beat while leading a jazz band called the Kansas City Seven. Eventually they became Locomotive, a group that would rattle through close to twenty members and everything from R&B and soul to ska and psychedelia during the course of the sixties.

By the summer of 1968 Simpson had packed in being a musician to manage Locomotive full time, making use of the contacts he had accumulated through gigging and photography. "The guys said to me, 'Why don't you concentrate on management?' It might have been their way of saying, 'Stop playing fucking trumpet,' but I'll never know." He called the company Big Bear, a nickname which John Peel had apparently adopted for him. Blues-rock trio Bakerloo joined the roster and then Tea and Symphony, an acid folk ensemble who had emerged from Moseley's hippie scene and built a following with a theatrical live set combining film projections, a light show and mime artist. "They were easier to get gigs for in the beginning, because they were so weird."

The final piece in the Big Bear jigsaw had been punters at the opening night of Henry's, a heavy blues act from Aston who started life as Polka Tulk (named after a Pakistani fabric shop, or perhaps a brand of talcum powder - such are the esoteric debates that bands generate when they become massive). By this point they were going under the name Earth, and they asked Simpson if they could play a set at the Crown. In September he put them on as support for Ten Years After - as legend has it, with four Henry's T-shirts as payment - and the crowd's response persuaded him to take them on. The photograph opposite was taken after one of their band meetings, on a grassy bank outside Simpson's house in Edgbaston.

All four bands were the products of an extremely fertile music scene. In Simpson's view, the number of ballrooms in the area helped lay the foundations in the early sixties. "Each of them had probably a 16-piece resident band, working five or six nights a week - and these weren't all Birmingham musicians, they came from all over the country." By the end of the decade the ballrooms had made way for the pub and college circuit and redevelopment had helped to scatter the audience, but the commitment to nonstop gigging endured with the support of receptive crowds. "Birmingham always seemed ready to give a band the benefit of the doubt."

The first of the Big Bear acts to make ripples nationally was Locomotive. Frontman and organist Norman Haines had developed a taste for blue beat and ska while working in a record shop just west of the city in Smethwick, and wrote a song which riffed on Desmond Dekker's '007'. 'Rudi's In Love' was picked up by one of Simpson's contacts, promoter Tony Hall, and the Parlophone release peaked in the charts at number 25 in October 1968. When Parlophone turned

Below: 1968 Henry's advert and Black Sabbath (Jim Simpson, c.1969)

Opposite: Henry's T-shirt (c.1968)

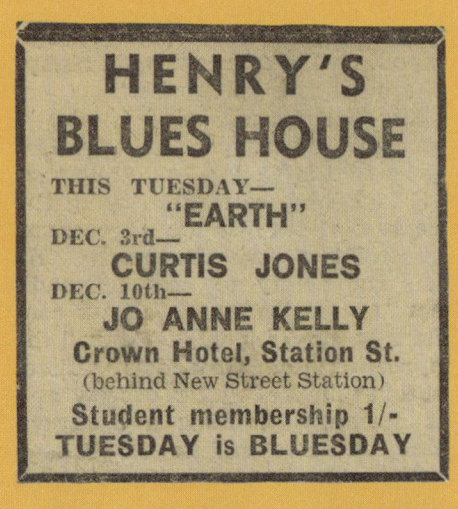

THIS WAY TO THE REVOLUTION

HENRY'S
BLUESHOUSE

BIG BEARS FFOLLY

**COLLEGE OF BUILDING & COMMERCE
STUDENTS UNION, CONCOURSE BUILDING
SHELTON, STOKE-ON-TRENT**

An Evening of Experience, Experiment & Blues

WEDNESDAY, 12th FEBRUARY, 1969

Compere
TONY HALL

★ THE LOCOMOTIVE
★ BAKERLOO BLUES LINE
★ TEA & SYMPHONY
★ EARTH
★ ROY EVERRETT & THE BLUES HOUNDS

8 p.m to 12 p.m.

Admission by Ticket only   Licensed Bar applied for

Tickets 10/- or on production of Students Union Card at College 7/6

Meet Big Bear Ffolly, the Birmingham multi-group outfit and Britain's answer to the Kasenetz-Katz Singing Orchestral Circus—though the Ffolly's music is more blues and progressive than the Circus' bubblegum pop. Earth, Bakerloo, Tea & Symphony and Locomotive, who had a recent Chart hit with "Rudi's In Love," are the four groups that make up the Ffolly. When performing together each band has its spot and all come together for a freewheeling "jam" at the end. The groups made their home town debut at Birmingham's Opposite Lock in January and make their London debut at the Marquee on February 6. Line up minus Tea and Symphony is (l to r) TERRY POOLE (Bakerloo), TONY IOMMI (Earth), TERRY BUTLER (E), BILL WARD (E), JOHN OSBOURNE (E), MICK HINCKS (Locomotive), CLEM CLEMPSON (B), JIM SIMPSON (their manager), NORMAN HAINES (L), ROY EVERETT (who sings solo), PETE YORK (B), and MIKE TAYLOR, BILL MADGE and BOB LAMB, all of Locomotive, whose new single is reviewed on page 6.

Festival
Big Bear Follies

UNION HALL   **7·30**
MARCH 2nd   **BAR**

Locomotive
Black Sabbath
Tea & Symphony

5/-

UNIVERSITY OF ASTON IN BIRMINGHAM GUILD OF STUDENTS

down the follow-up, Christmas novelty tune 'Rudi the Red-Nosed Reindeer,' Simpson set up his own Big Bear label to release it under the alias of Steam Shovel.

In the meantime Tea and Symphony were playing Strange Days events in support of the nascent Arts Lab, and Earth had graduated to larger gigs including support slots at Mothers. After being poached by rock flautist Ian Anderson for a week-long stint with Jethro Tull at the end of 1968, lead guitarist Tony Iommi came back down to Earth/Birmingham aware of the work ethic that would be required for success. The group were leaving behind their blues roots to develop something new; a hard, propulsive sound built around heavy riffs, and lyrics by bassist Geezer Butler which mixed the pastoral and the satanic along with elements of science fiction and anti-war polemic. A Mario Bava horror film provided the title for one of their early songs, and by the summer of 1969 Black Sabbath would be adopted as the group's name.

Before then all four of Simpson's acts hit the road for a brief package tour of the UK. "The London media were ignoring all the bands, and we just felt defiant. Big Bear Ffolly was a way of showing the world what quality music was around here." Each act had its own spot, and then the show would culminate in an extended jam which reflected the cross-fertilisation between the groups at this time. Norman Haines would go on to record early Sabbath demos of his own songs, while Sabbath's Bill Ward occasionally stood in on drums for Bakerloo, and at some point all four acts worked with producer Gus Dudgeon - better known for 'Space Oddity', and his work with Elton John.

Both Bakerloo and Tea and Symphony had Dudgeon-recorded albums in the pipeline on EMI's Harvest label, recently set up to accommodate the explosion in progressive music. By the time Bakerloo's LP came out the band itself had broken up, while Tea and Symphony's debut achieved the kind of limited mainstream acceptance that you would expect from an album called *An Asylum for the Musically Insane*. A lysergic, vaudevillian wig-out, it offers some idea of the band's mixed-media stage shows and has since been rediscovered as a proto-prog milestone with original pressings of the record fetching hundreds of pounds. Locomotive's first album *We Are Everything You See* spent all of 1969 in limbo, victim of a stand-off between Parlophone and the band who refused to retain the ska template of their solitary hit and instead recorded two sides of jazzy psychedelia. When it finally came out on 1 February 1970, it disappeared without trace.

Two weeks later on Friday 13th, Black Sabbath's eponymous debut was released and went straight to number 8 in the UK album charts. Recorded the previous autumn in a single day, it captured the stripped-down sound which the group had perfected through endless touring, and its doom-laden atmosphere seemed to chime better with the zeitgeist than the work of their trippier stable-mates. Fourteen labels had turned it down before Vertigo took it, and apart from a session on John Peel's *Top Gear* radio show it had received very little media exposure. In interviews Simpson emphasised the organic, homegrown nature of the band's success, an implicit dig at their more carefully constructed contemporaries Led Zeppelin.

Having a hit required a change of approach, the manager no

Previous page: 1969 Big Bears Ffolly advert, 1969 newspaper report and 1970 poster

Below: Three incarnations of Locomotive from 1965 (with poet Roy Fisher on piano), 1967 (with Jim Simpson on the right) and 1969 (with Norman Haines second on the left)

Opposite: Cover of Jo Sago by Tea and Symphony (Harvest, 1970)

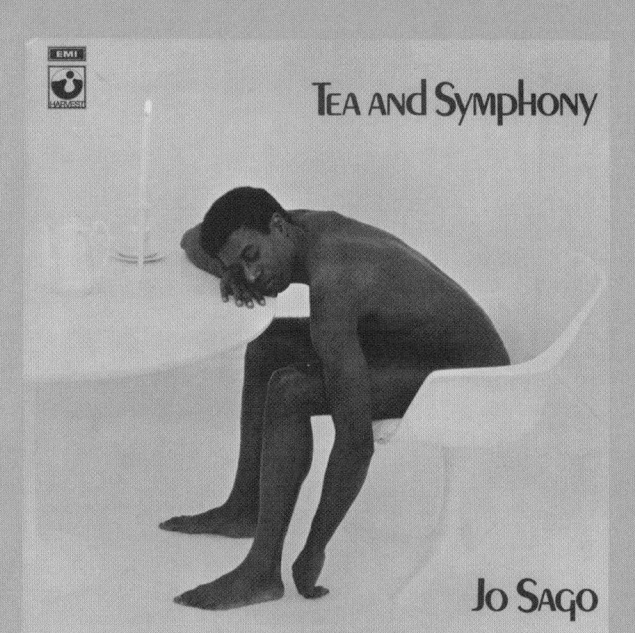

longer driving the group back from gigs but instead staying in the office at home to field a growing volume of international calls. "They were queueing up to buy off me... I thought [the band would] understand that we were going places." However, Sabbath became convinced that Big Bear could only take them so far, and that summer they were wooed by former Don Arden associate Patrick Meehan with promises of big money deals and breaking America. In September 1970, with their second album *Paranoid* about to reach number one and two years after they had first played at Henry's, Black Sabbath sacked Jim Simpson.

By the end of the year the original Ffolly foursome had either disbanded or - in Sabbath's case - defected, but there was one more record to emerge. Although *An Asylum...* had not been a big seller, Tea and Symphony were able to release a follow-up on Harvest. *Jo Sago - A Play on Music* was a concept album, its first side a song series narrating the misadventures of a young man from the Caribbean living on Balsall Heath's Ladypool Road: "His world isn't where it should be - it's somewhere in between." The sleeve notes described the changes wrought to the neighbourhood by immigration, changes which "drove the less adaptable residents and their Colonial memories away from the parish, and overnight their scuttled mansions became adventure playgrounds for Jo Sago, his friends and others like him." Like 'Rudi's in Love,' it's an example of how Birmingham's white, male rock scene absorbed and appropriated black influences - not just from the Deep South or Chicago, but from their own doorstep.

In the seventies Big Bear would shift their focus away from rock, mounting a number of UK tours for American blues performers including Lightnin' Slim, Eddie 'Guitar' Burns and Doctor Ross - many of them consigned to obscurity and low-waged jobs at the time. Later the company would establish a jazz festival in Birmingham which was about to mark its 35th edition when I visited their offices on the Hagley Road. Down an alley, through a rusty metal door and up a winding staircase, this is an authentic time-capsule piled high with the remnants of half a century in the music business. Among the commemorative bow-ties and contact sheets, a scrapbook of Black Sabbath cuttings charts the evolution from Henry's to cocaine mania, including a 1973 article in which Patrick Meehan shows off his new sports car. (The band subsequently spent some years pursuing Meehan through the courts.)

For all of Big Bear's other achievements Simpson will forever have 'Black Sabbath's first manager' near the top of his CV, and he remains a little wistful when talking about them: "like losing your best girl." As we pull this book together, an exhibition devoted to the band and their enduring influence is being installed at Birmingham Museum & Art Gallery, while Sabbath lookalikes and soundalikes seem more numerous than ever. Heavy industry will always get a mention in the band's origin myth - particularly the well-worn tale of Tony losing two fingertips in a sheet-metal press - but it's clear that the musical ferment of late sixties Birmingham also played its part in producing this unlikely, world-conquering export.

THE BIRMINGHAM INNER CIRCLE

Although he has had a varied career spanning over fifty years, for many people Nick Hedges will forever be associated with the photographs he took for Shelter as a recent graduate in the late 60s and early 70s. Starting out in Birmingham and moving on to other UK cities including Glasgow, Bradford and London, his camera recorded horrific housing conditions and families at the end of their tether, forming the central part of a hugely effective campaign. When talking about Janet Mendelsohn's images of Balsall Heath I had got into the habit of contrasting their world-view with portraits taken in the same neighbourhood by Hedges; the one full of warmth and cheery resilience, the other a realm of hopeless victims pinned down by damp and vermin. But of course those Shelter images had a particular job to do. When I went to meet Nick Hedges at home in Shrewsbury and had a chance to dig through the work he did while studying in Birmingham between 1966 and 1968, I discovered far more light and shade.

HOT JAZZ HERE
JAZZ

DOUBLE DIAMOND
BREW XI
New Street Station

A grammar-school boy from Bromsgrove, Hedges credits his own political awakening to the influence of civil rights and Vietnam, as well as to an aunt who took him on CND marches as a kid. "You gradually become radicalised without knowing it - it's just a natural suit to wear." While his peers were learning to play guitar he discovered a love of photography, and in 1965 he got a place at Birmingham College of Art. After suburban Worcestershire the buzz and cultural mix of Handsworth "felt like liberation", and one of his first college projects was recording a jazz gig in the Cross Guns pub around the corner from his flat. Working with a Leica Rangefinder to minimise noise and make the most of available light, he settled on a low-key approach that has served him well ever since. "What I always try and do is enter into an agreement with the people that I'm photographing: 'This is what I'm doing, this is why, would you mind?' So they know I'm taking photographs, but they forget about it - I just become insignificant."

The number eight inner circle bus route became an essential tool for Hedges on his voyage of discovery, documenting a huge range of subjects across the city. The early part of 1966 was spent following Labour's Smethwick candidate Andrew Faulds in his ultimately successful campaign to unseat Conservative MP Peter Griffiths, while elsewhere in the negatives you can find Blues matches, snooker halls, Guy Fawkes bonfires and snowball fights. A handful of street shots were used by Oxford University Press for Rex and Moore's landmark sociology work *Race, Community and Conflict: A Study of Sparkbrook*, and then towards the end of his second year Hedges had the rug pulled out from under him. The principal announced that the college would be unable to support his photojournalistic aspirations in the final year, and that there was no point in him continuing his studies. "I was absolutely dumbfounded."

An unhappy period followed working as a studio assistant in London and a 'chain boy' on the new M5 motorway, before a change of leadership at the college opened up a route for him to return to Birmingham and complete the final year of his diploma. In the autumn of 1967 Hedges began to work his way steadily through a series of projects and assignments: "I was quite determined to make good use of my time having been kicked out." These included a study of the Newtown Palace, a dilapidated picturehouse that had begun to screen South Asian movies, and in May 1968 a record of a tense rally held in Victoria Square shortly after Enoch Powell's speech at the Midland Hotel. The combustible atmosphere was also affecting the college itself, and the following month a group of students inspired by the example of Hornsey College of Art and *les événements* in Paris decided to occupy the union building: "they'd had enough of the Vietnam War, and they'd had enough of being treated like children by college management."

This presented Hedges with a dilemma, as he was on a deadline to complete a large commission for the Birmingham Housing Trust. "So at night I would sleep at the student union - I actually met a girlfriend, that was a bonus - and in the daytime I was out photographing the city." The resulting images take us on a tour of the inner ring's housing crisis, documenting the bleak circumstances which families had to contend with in these condemned neighbourhoods along with moments of humour and intimacy. Already the photographer was beginning to wonder whether charity was a salve to liberal consciences which was preventing more fundamental change from happening. "I put this to David Mumford, who chaired the housing trust. He said 'Look Nick, last week I had a married couple with four children. They turned up on the doorstep about 4:30 on a Thursday afternoon. They'd got nowhere to live. What should I do? Shall I say I can't help you today, but if you come back in two years the revolution may have happened?'"

In August the photographs were exhibited as two-metre prints at the Birmingham Housing Trust's offices. On a visit to the trust Shelter Director Des Wilson happened to see the show, and shortly afterwards he rang Hedges to ask if he'd like to join the charity in London as their in-house photographer. The role took him all over the country, although one of his first assignments was back in Balsall Heath in early 1969. The resulting images of the Milne family on Vincent Crescent helped feed into a media storm about living conditions on the street, with a 1970 public housing report detailing the extent of damp and infestation and concluding: "Vincent Crescent is dead; the houses should be buried without further ceremony or delay. There will be few mourners." The street was demolished shortly afterwards.

When asked by the Guardian in 2009 to pick his favourite shot, Nick Hedges went back to an image of the double-bass player at the Cross Guns. It's clear that this period helped to shape everything he has done since. "I think I was extremely lucky to be in the city at the point at which so much was changing... If I'd been there a few years earlier, it would have been locked into a post-war freezer where nothing had happened yet. If I'd been there ten years later, the old inner core of the city would've vanished. I also feel very grateful for my experience in meeting so many different communities. It made me a much more rounded human."

Previous page: Nick Hedges (Maggie Gathercole, 1967). Opposite: Constitution Hill and the Rotunda (Nick Hedges, 1966/7)

CROSS GUNS PUB, SOHO ROAD, HANDSWORTH, 1966

"It was a relaxed situation - the people were generous in allowing me to do it. I was able to move around the pub in a completely free way."

Caribbean jazz quartet at the Cross Guns pub in Handsworth (Nick Hedges, 1966)

91

NEWTOWN PALACE CINEMA, NEW TOWN ROW, NEWTOWN, 1967

"It was absolutely buzzing. There was no provision in the city for any kind of cultural life for Asian families, other than the temple or mosque. It was threadbare, the culture. You used to get guys turning up at the cinema with reel-to-reel tape recorders, to record the soundtrack of the film they were watching."

Newtown Palace cinema (Nick Hedges, 1967)

THIS WAY TO THE REVOLUTION

BIRMINGHAM HOUSING TRUST COMMISSION, COMPLETED IN SUMMER 1968

Above: Tower blocks in Nechells Green. Below: Mr Sar and his sons at bathtime in Balsall Heath (Nick Hedges, 1968)

"The whole of the inner ring was being decimated; it was like a mouth full of bad teeth. Ladywood, Hockley, Aston, Saltley, Sparkbrook, Balsall Heath... that whole crescent was in the process of being demolished and rebuilt, and people were left in a state of limbo for years."

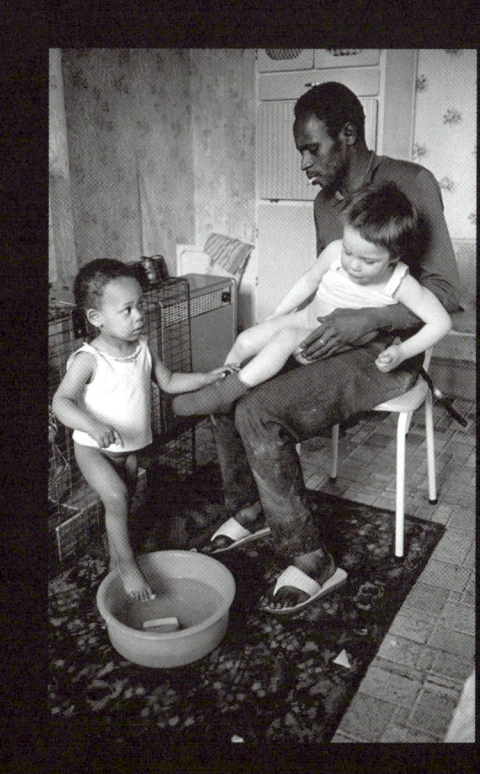

THE BIRMINGHAM INNER CIRCLE

BLACK AND WHITE UNITE AND FIGHT

It's a crisp, warm Sunday afternoon in central Birmingham. Demonstrators are filing into Victoria Square in anticipation of a visit from Prime Minister Harold Wilson, due to give a speech in the Town Hall at 3pm. There's an eclectic array of placards on display: students in donkey-jackets proclaim 'Yankee Aggressors Out of Vietnam' and 'Wilson is an Optical Illusion'; smarter and more orderly, a large group of Indian and Pakistani workers carry signs reading 'Black and White Unite and Fight' and 'Prosecute Fascist Powell'; bringing up the rear, a group of dancing, singing African protestors attack the 'Nigerian genocide' in Biafra. There's a large crowd of curious onlookers, from school-kids to old ladies, and on Galloways Corner at the top of the square a pocket of fascists is chanting "Send 'em back!" Among them is Colin Jordan, a former Coventry school teacher and prominent British nationalist.

On Wilson's arrival the atmosphere audibly changes. We see him escorted between the Town Hall and Council House to a chorus of booing and shouting, while a police cordon attempts to hold back demonstrators. There are flare-ups between the different factions. A police line stands between students and Asian workers on one side and Powell supporters on the other. An older man with a Brummie accent is getting increasingly agitated and gestures towards the Council House: "You've got Wilson behind you, a black-lover. If Powell was Prime Minister... he'd bin the lot of you." One student protestor says to the police "aren't you going to help us?" In the wake of Wilson's departure things begin to fragment. Some protestors are led away. Another placard: 'Would You Let Enoch Powell Marry Your Daughter?' Jordan is hoisted up on the shoulders of some of his supporters, amidst tentative Nazi salutes. A big group of Asian workers is dispersed (some would say shoved) down the hill towards Pinfold Street by the police.

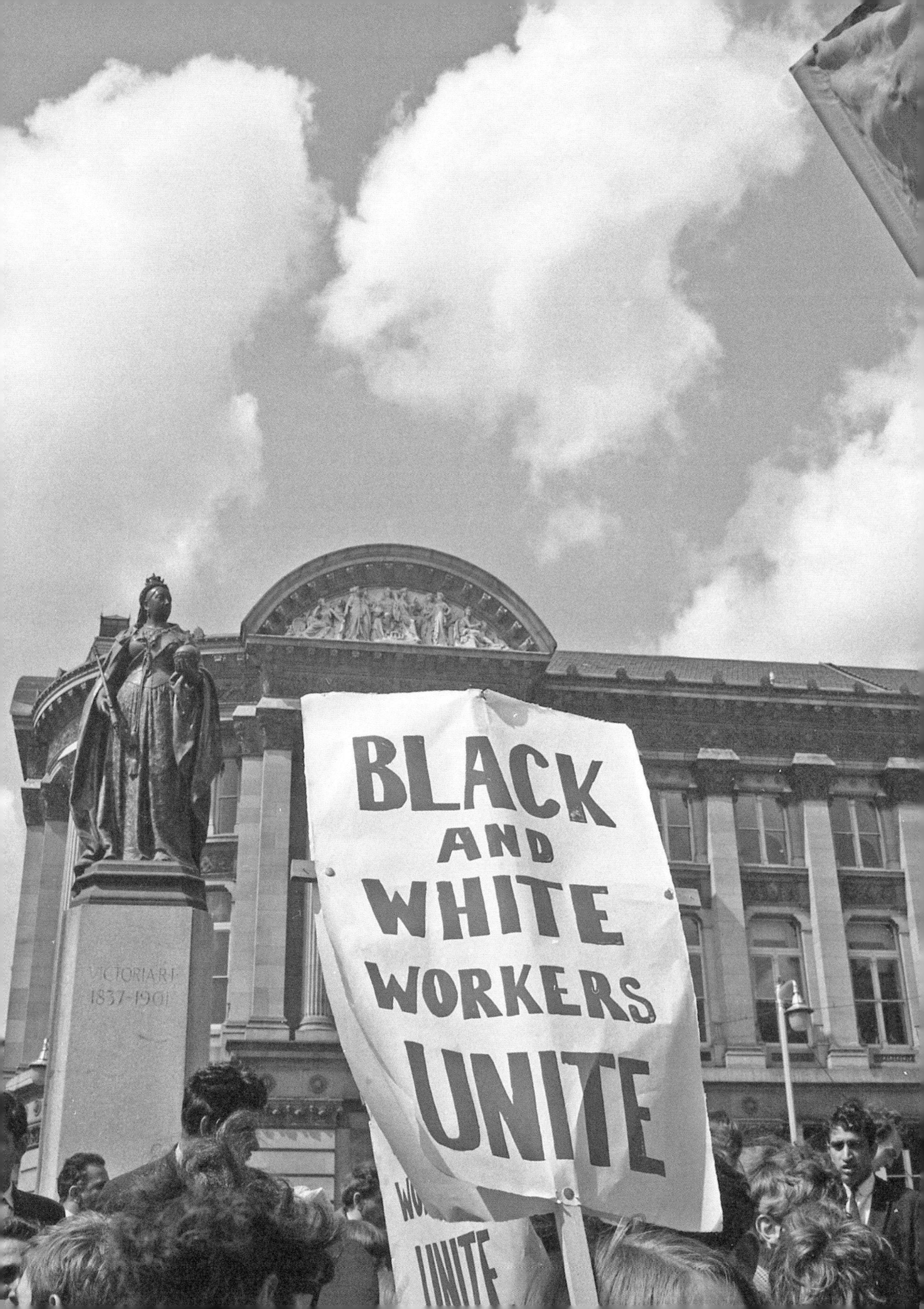
BLACK AND WHITE WORKERS UNITE
VICTORIA R I
1837-1901
UNITE

BLACK AND WHITE UNITE AND FIGHT

This footage came to light during our research, unseen since it was filmed by an ATV news cameraman on 5 May, 1968. It's about 16 minutes worth of rushes from the 'Black and White Unite and Fight' demo, which had been organised by the Indian Workers' Association in response both to Wilson's visit and also to Enoch Powell's speech at the Midland Hotel a couple of weeks previously. Although Wilson defined himself against Powell that day - "I am not prepared to stand aside and see this country engulfed by the racial conflict which calculated orators or ignorant prejudice can create" - his own Labour administration had been in power for four years, and their record on race relations was seen as distinctly patchy. Many attacked the timidity of their 1965 Race Relations Bill, which failed to outlaw racial discrimination within the most contentious areas of housing and employment. Having in opposition decried the Tories' Commonwealth Immigration Act, designed to limit the number of people arriving from Britain's former colonies, in early 1968 Wilson's government actually strengthened the Act with the 'grandparent rule', in response to fears of an influx of Kenyan Asians. There was a clear sense within both of the main parties that standing up for the rights of immigrants was not a vote-winner, also reflected on a local level. In *Second City Politics*, Kenneth Newton detailed the levels of ignorance and bigotry among Birmingham councillors at this time and concluded: "Race relations in Birmingham has been half a political issue because only half the case has been put - the case of coloured immigrants has yet to see the light of day as a force in local affairs."

One of those attempting to address this vacuum in the late sixties was Avtar Singh Jouhl, an organiser of the 5 May march. He had arrived in Smethwick ten years previously from a farming background in Djalandar. Like many others he had grown up on rosy images of the UK and was dismayed by the smog and poor conditions he encountered, particularly after starting work at Shotton Brothers foundry in Oldbury. Having already been involved in student politics in the Punjab he soon joined the Indian Workers' Association, a UK-based left wing organisation which had formed in the 1930s to support India's fight for independence. By the late 1950s their focus was on tackling the discrimination faced by migrant workers, from lobbying for equal pay to protesting the widespread colour bar which could be found among shops, cafés and rental accommodation at the time. At one point Jouhl, by then the group's national General Secretary, was arrested and later cleared after refusing to leave a Black Country pub on the grounds of his skin colour.

The 1964 election established Smethwick as a symbolic battleground in this fight. Bucking the national trend, local Conservative candidate Peter Griffiths unseated Labour MP Patrick Gordon Walker with the help of some inflammatory anti-immigration rhetoric later attributed to Colin Jordan and fellow nationalists. Having been closely involved in the counter-campaign, the IWA then managed to secure the visit of Malcolm X a few months later, a PR coup which briefly put Smethwick in the media spotlight. Jouhl: "Malcolm came out very clearly on questions of power and exploitation. He would be considered an extremist to those who were practising racism, but to black and Asian people his visit was an act of solidarity." The alliances with black activists and student groups which Jouhl and his comrades forged at this time would prove vital when they were planning the Wilson rally in 1968.

On the day of the protest Jouhl came straight from his brother-in-law's wedding. The police were keen to keep marchers away from Town Hall, and sent them on a route around the city centre while Wilson was speaking. Some returned to the square once the march had ended, and as the ATV footage shows they received far more attention from the police than the fascists did. Shortly after the cameras stopped rolling things became more heated on Pinfold Street and IWA leaders Jagmohan Joshi and Sohan Singh Sandhu were arrested and bundled into a van. In Jouhl's account: "I was appealing to the demonstrators in Punjabi - 'don't worry, we will get them bailed out' - and when I was making this announcement two policemen arrested me. They didn't know what I was saying and thought I was inciting the demonstration against the police." Jouhl joined his comrades at Steelhouse Lane police station, and the following day was charged with disorderly conduct. The magistrate dismissed the charge: "The accused seems to have taken a responsible view of his duties as the organiser of a demonstration. It is not impossible that he became excited, and there may have been some misunderstanding as he was talking in a foreign tongue."

Also in court was Frederick Haywood of Handsworth, who on being fined £5 for a disorderly act responded: "The way I see it, fighting Fascism should be commended not penalised." In total ten were arrested at the protest, including a couple of IWA members who had to be treated in hospital for injuries which they alleged had been caused by the arresting officers. Joshi attempted to bring a case of police brutality, describing the course of events in a letter to the Home Office along with a more general concern about "the indifference of the police to attacks on coloured workers, police discrimination against them and also police provocation of coloured people." In a reply David Ennals wrote that there was no case to answer, and that "the Chief Constable of Birmingham is satisfied that the police acted with admirable restraint and tolerance throughout." When Jouhl attempted to organise a similar protest the following summer, he remembers being advised by the Superintendent: "be very careful Mr Jouhl - last time you got off, but next time we will make sure you don't."

"We do not sit back, we hit back" is a phrase that recurs in IWA literature and speeches of the time, reflecting the influence of Malcolm X and subsequent black activism, particularly in the wake of Martin Luther King's assassination. The association was increasingly disillusioned with a legislative and lobbying approach which seemed to have brought limited progress, and in the wake of Powell's speech there was a renewed appetite among black and Asian groups to make common cause. On 29 April over 50 organisations including the IWA signed a Declaration of Black Unity at a house in Leamington, the same house which had a burning cross nailed to its door by a short-lived attempt at a Ku Klux Klan chapter a couple of years before. By December an audience of over a thousand - predominantly Asian men - gathered at Town Hall for a Black Youth conference organised by Mihir Gupta. Along with guest speakers including Tariq Ali the Evening Mail announced a musical programme which would feature "Negro vocals, and possibly a sitar recital." On the podium Gupta advised: "If a white man slaps you, slap back... The days of turning the other cheek are over." Gerry Archer of the West Indian People's Union remembered the Birmingham that he arrived in during the early 1950s as "a broken-down, bomb-damaged shambles of a city... Today we have the second most modern city in the country. Whose labour built this? Ours. What do we hear from the racialist Birmingham City Council? 'We will put up check-points at the entrance to see that no more immigrants arrive in the city.' That is a good thank you for what we have done for them!"

Unable to contain a diversity of moderate and radical voices, the alliance struggled to sustain itself for long, but this period marked a step away from the rhetoric of cultural assimilation towards an emphasis on plurality and equal rights. Reflecting back fifty years later, Avtar Singh Jouhl saw it as "an important chapter in the struggle... for the generations born afterwards, they didn't experience the cruel type of discrimination we experienced during the 50s and 60s." However, speaking a few days after Boris Johnson had likened Muslim women to "bank-robbers" and "letter-boxes," he was also confident that some things do not change: "In every stage, you've got no alternative but to fight. Unless you fight back they will win, like the Nazis won in Germany." Along with others we spoke to, Jouhl felt that narratives of 1968 had been skewed by a preoccupation with 'Rivers of Blood'. "Enoch Powell's speech remains up on the wall for people to remember. Many incidents or events are not up on the wall."

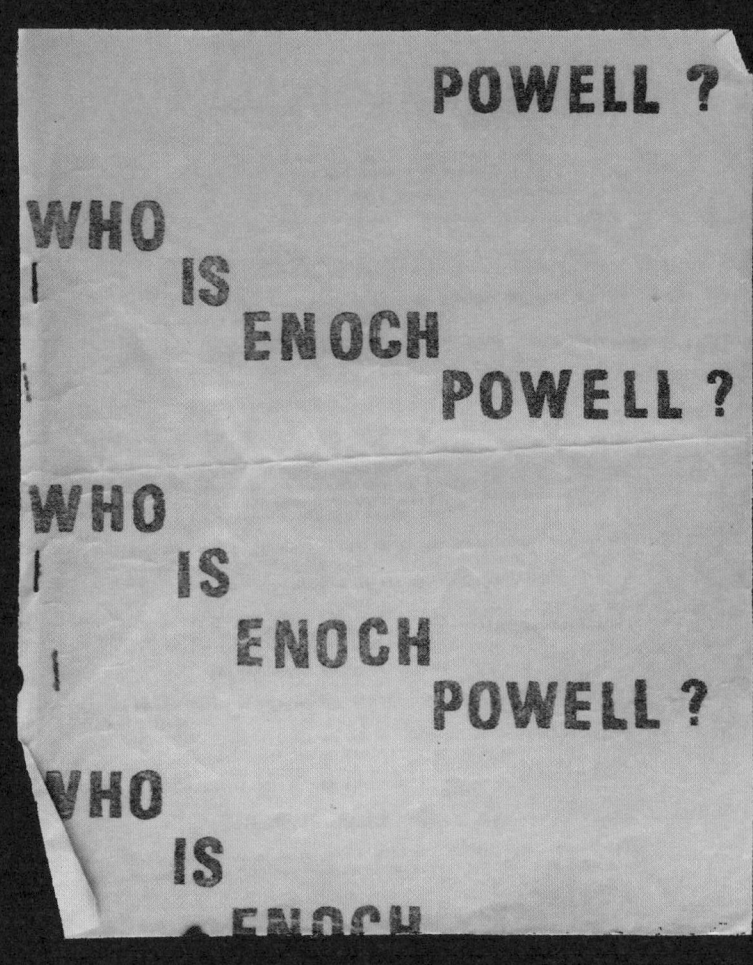

Previous page: Images of the Victoria Square rally, including Harold Wilson speaking inside Town Hall (Nick Hedges, 1968)

Above: Cover of campaign leaflet (Indian Workers' Association, 1968)

THE JOURNEY BACK

By Abdullah Hussein

We all came together for two activities on a Sunday. The first was going to the movies. The Sikh residents rented out a theatre in the neighbourhood and showed our desi films. Altogether there were two films and four shows. Later they bought the place and ran films seven days a week. Our entire community turned up there. People rushed through whatever they were doing. Even the sick came crawling out of their beds at the prospect. A few hundred people would show up. Seeing a film isn't such a big thing now. We are free to go see whatever movie we want - English, German, American - movies that take your breath away and make your head spin. Back then though, the movie used to be the highlight of the week. We waited for it all week long. After lunch we changed into fresh clothes and gathered in one of the Mirpuri rooms downstairs. The show began at four o'clock and we had fixed three o'clock as the time of our grand departure. At a quarter to three, we would begin hollering at the dawdlers to hurry up. There was no question at all about going there in twos and fours, we always went en masse. There was safety in numbers.

At precisely three o'clock, thirteen of us filed out in our well-ironed, clean clothes and shining boots and marched off to the movies. There would be droves of people everywhere heading towards the theatre at that time, making it impossible for the police, or any other white man, to figure out who was a legal alien and who was an illegal one. All they knew was that today was our movie day and they could expect a large crowd.

A few hundred of us paraded right through white territory down to that movie theatre. And we wore whatever pleased us - coat and pants, pyjama, shalwar-kurta - anything. You could hear the Urdu and Punjabi film songs blaring from loudspeakers blocks away... Some of the whites passing by would stop and stare at us. A couple of policemen always hung around to keep things in order, but they stood quietly to one side. Sometimes, when a really popular film came along, a near riot would break out over buying tickets. That got the police into action. They'd wave their arms and shout to restore peace, but they never used their batons.

A completely different scene awaited you in the theatre hall. Popular film songs sung by Lata Mangeshkar, Mohammed Rafi, Nur Jahan, and others greeted you. And when the film started it put you back in a familiar world - your own movie stars, your own language, dances, songs, jokes, the same storyline, the same scenes - you felt as if you had never left your country.

Ah, the films! Pretty strange things. Often I would be so absorbed in the story that I wouldn't know where I was until the lights came on, and even then it took a few seconds to reorient myself. It was an odd feeling. Lots of people cried at the tearkerkers - the crescendo of sniffles told you that. But me, I never cried. No matter how involved I got in a picture, I never forgot that it was only a story. I did learn something interesting by going there - one grows tender hearted when far from home. We thought about our homes, wives and children constantly - the very same things we never much concerned ourselves with before.

Going over those memories was like cutting our hearts out. You could marry and raise a family here, but where would you get the satisfaction of speaking your native tongue? Our speech, gait, clothes, long sunny days, the sounds and smells of home, the gentle touch - these things just don't exist here. I tell you, I've seen big, solid men with skill and plenty of money break down and cry their hearts out at these movies, as if they were suddenly told they were stricken with some incurable disease. When the theatre lights came on at the end of the film, you could see everyone's face radiating with satisfaction, which however didn't last long. It was already dimmed by the time they had reached the exit. On the way back we talked about the movie and repeated its jokes. And so a weekly event would pass by.

Text: Excerpt from 'The Journey Back' by Abdullah Hussein, trans. Muhammad Umar Memon.
Published in *Stories of Exile and Alienation* (Oxford University Press, Karachi, 1998)

Newtown Palace cinema (Nick Hedges, 1967)

Abdullah Hussein was born in 1931 in Rawalpindi, then part of India. While working in the laboratory of a cement factory in the Punjab he wrote his first novel in Urdu, a historical saga spanning the period from the First World War to the aftermath of Partition, and on publication in 1963 *Udaas Naslen* (*The Weary Generations*) quickly became a bestseller in Pakistan. Soon afterwards he had turned his back on writing and moved to England, taking a series of jobs at restaurants and petrol stations before ending up at the North Thames Gas Board for several years. This period in England inspired a series of later writings about exile and alienation including the novella 'Wapsi ka Safar' ('The Journey Back,' 1981), which drew on Hussein's time in multi-occupancy lodgings in Birmingham in the late 1960s and was later adapted into the film *Brothers in Trouble* (dir: Udayan Prasad, 1995). One sequence in the book describes a Sunday afternoon ritual.

OCCUPATION

BY EDWARD JACKSON

TONIGHT!

Under the paving-stones, the beach! Or, at least, better student representation on university administrative bodies. When University of Birmingham students made the decision to occupy key buildings on campus in November 1968, the tumult of Paris five or so months earlier had certainly cooled. Further afield, the chaos of the Democratic National Convention had only encouraged America's silent majority to elect Richard Nixon as president. Everywhere, it seemed, the clamp was starting to come down, a long hot summer of revolt giving way to the first intimations of backlash. However, this only makes the actions taken at the University of Birmingham all the more remarkable. As the decade's last major student protest (at least, within the UK), the occupation of the Great Hall and the Vice-Chancellor's office towards the end of 1968 brought the entire institution to a moment of crisis.

Student uprisings weren't new to UK universities by this point. From 1966 onwards sit-ins had rocked the LSE, Leicester, Essex, and closer to home, Aston. That said, Birmingham was a unique case: as then Guild President Ray Phillips reflects, "the sheer level of activity at Birmingham was much, much greater than anywhere else." At the final general meeting of December 5th which ended the sit-in, over 4,000 students were present, so many that it had to take place outside - an impressive number given that the student population at the time numbered around 6,000. "It was a wake-up call to the university," former Guild Secretary Chris Tyrrell notes, but why were authorities so asleep at the wheel when it came to student grievances? Untangling exactly why the sit-in happened is tricky, but as good place to start as any is The Student Role, the first spark in a long fuse towards occupation.

The Build Up

"The Guild of Students had produced a document called The Student Role, which outlined why students should be involved in the running of the university", remembers Anne Durbin (*née* Naylor), a participant of the sit-in and later Guild President. However, as The Student Role continued to bounce between various administrative bodies, "students were really being excluded from the discussions... It was felt that the university was minimising their involvement and taking decisions about it behind closed doors." By shutting students out from debating a document that - ironically - was all about their greater inclusion in deciding how the university operated, the authorities made the first of many missteps that would result in undergraduates eating fish and chips on the Vice-Chancellor's carpet.

The Student Role, then, encapsulated a broader discontent with the university's stolid ethos. But other factors were also important: in Tyrrell's words, "you have to see the sit-in as... the culmination of a number of other activities that had taken place on the campus," whether those were ongoing disputes over the running of the Refectory, or protests against a visit from Enoch Powell. Indeed, 1968 saw students formulating radical critiques of the institution's bureaucratic fustiness. For instance, an article titled 'The Concept of the University', in the spring 1968 edition of university magazine Mermaid, complained that the place "operates without coherent direction, its professors... rusted away in office. Student representation might not only make the system more democratic, but also more sane."

When it came to the figurehead of student resentment though - the Vice-Chancellor - it wasn't rustiness so much as inexperience that was the problem. After the retirement of the well-liked Sir Robert Aitken in September 1968, Robert Brockie Hunter took up the position, a Scot whose main claim to fame was serving as General Montgomery's doctor during the war. As former student John Butcher reflects, "the authorities' position was 'students are here today, gone tomorrow - so if we fudge everything it won't be a problem'". With academic firebrands like Stuart Hall and Dick Atkinson stirring student activity, though, fudging was not going to cut it. By the start of the autumn term, something big was on the horizon. In occupier Jenny Wickham's words, "it was a big upwelling of 'we're just not having this – this is just not how it's going to be'. That's what led to the sit-in."

Previous page: Vote to end the Great Hall occupation, held outside Birmingham University library (FW Rushton, 1968)

Below: Cover of Redbrick on 27 November 1968

Opposite: pre-occupation flyer

Following page: 'This Way To The Revolution' occupation sign

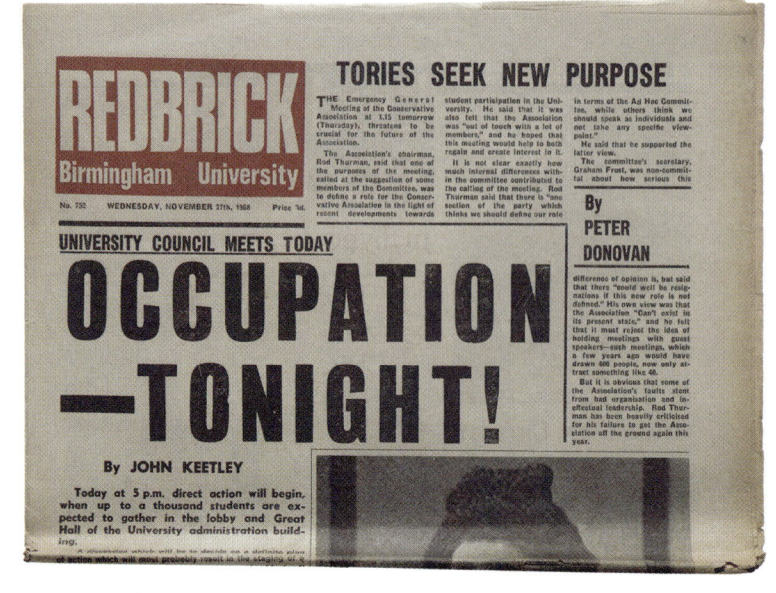

ACTION

WE HAVE HAD ENOUGH
SHABBY TREATMENT

THURSDAY 1-15
in
DEBATING HALL

Printed by Printcraft Press (Hednesford) Limited, 55 Market Street, Hednesford, Staffs.

THE TIMES MONDAY NOVEMBER 11 1968

LONDON STOCK EXCHANGE PRICES

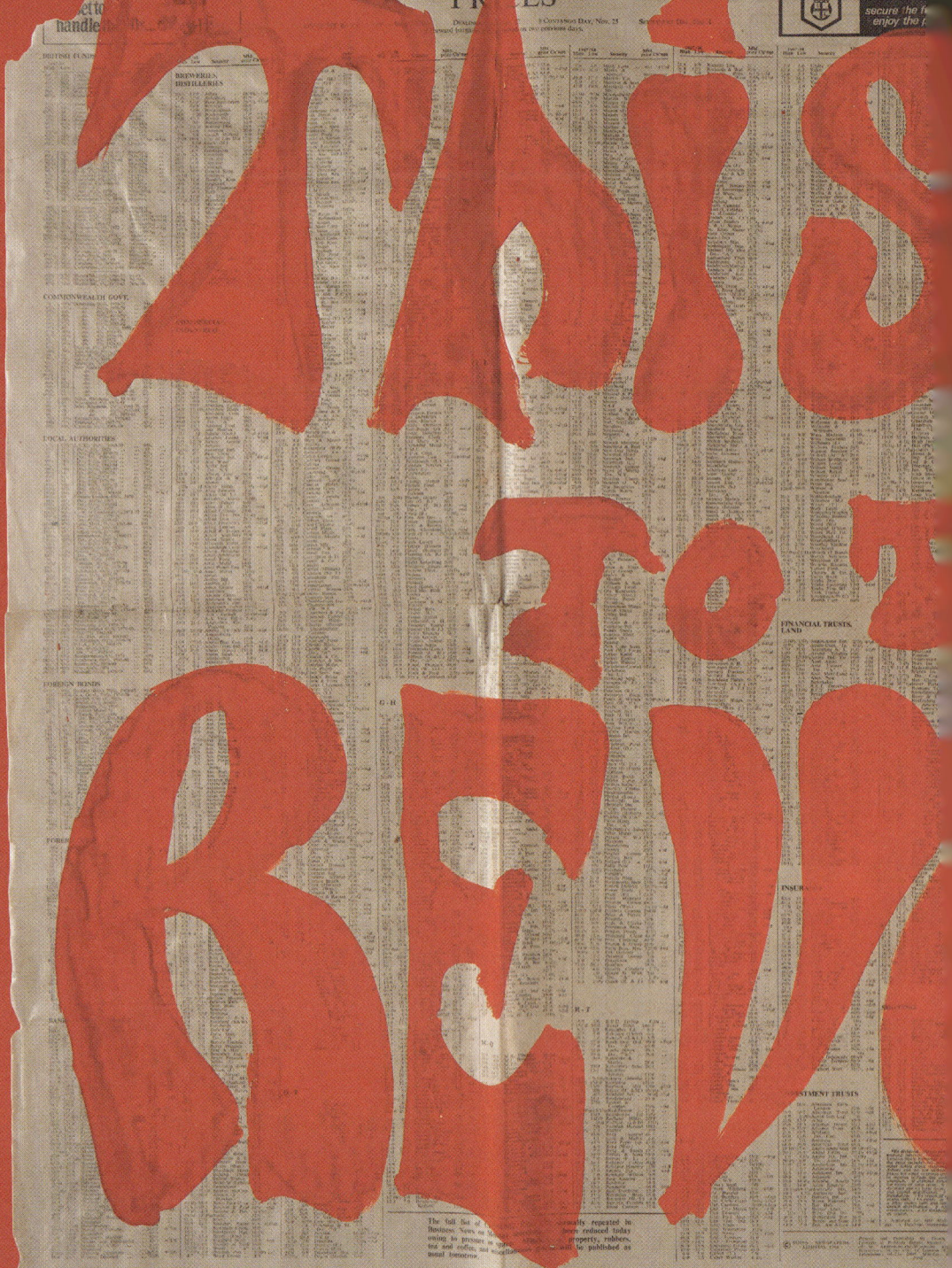

THE TIMES BUSINESS NEWS

MONDAY NOVEMBER 11 1968

American tax rise possible
By ROBERT JONES

Whitehall moves likely in bid to boost export drive
By MAURICE CORINA

Big safety setback for Rootes in US
By GILES SMITH

BOAC expects £12m operating surplus
By ARTHUR REED, Air Correspondent

Do you know of a better non-vintage Port than Taylor's Vintage Reserve?

TAYLOR'S VINTAGE RESERVE PORT

The Sit-In

The direct action originally mooted was more drastic: demonstrations and a mass strike. As the 30 October issue of university newspaper Redbrick relates, at a Guild Council meeting the preceding night "three hours of heated argument" led Sue Jackson, the Vice President of the Guild, to propose direct action if The Student Role was not accepted in its entirety by the end of November. "When asked precisely what she meant by 'direct action,' she replied, 'I mean strike, I mean blow the place up,' at which point Council erupted in applause and stamping." As Jackson's incendiary sentiments suggest, anger was reaching boiling point. But how did events actually play out?

As the Guild still debated what to do in light of the administration's poor handling of The Student Role, Durbin explains how "another group was set up sort of separate from the Guild council which was more radical, and they were keen for things to move faster." This ginger group's readiness to occupy forced the Guild into action, and on the afternoon of 28 November, it voted to join the fray. Immediately thereafter, 1,000 students made the short walk from the Union to the Great Hall and Aston Webb building, where they would stay for the next eight days. Luck also played a part, for, as Tyrrell notes, "the Vice-Chancellor left the window open, which gave us access to his office." The sit-in had begun.

Four demands were front and centre: acceptance of The Student Role; no victimisation of students involved; the creation of a commission to look at the university's structure; and the opening up of all university committees. Practicalities of food and sleep had to be met first, though: "I remember people coming with those big baker's plastic trays, walking in with trays of bacon sandwiches," recalls Wickham. "I slept a night in the Vice-Chancellor's office area," and "one or two nights in the Great Hall - we didn't have any bedding really, just slept on a coat or something. The Great Hall was hard." Austere conditions, perhaps, but the sit-in generally struck a good balance between hard work and conviviality. After waking up to The Beatles' 'Revolution' coming out of the loudspeakers, the rebels kept themselves busy with discussion groups, a teach-in, dancing, and leaflet and poster production.

In fact, as sit-ins go this one was particularly well-behaved. In addition to a Sunday service held for practising Christians, Wickham reflects that "there was no damage to the fabric of the building. We were mostly nice middle-class kids. Even if we were doing something revolutionary." Phillips agrees: "there was no sort of violence in any sense with a capital 'V' - we argued our way through things." Even so, local papers such as the Sunday Mercury and Evening Mail were generally hostile. A piece called 'Tell Me Lies About Birmingham' in Redbrick from the time observed that "a false image of students as 'long-haired layabouts' and 'bearded militants' has been constantly directed at the public." In the battle for public perception, then, the occupiers were quite isolated in their cause.

Student enthusiasm nonetheless swelled when the authorities made the tactical blunder of threatening reprisals. In Durbin's words, "all that did was to solidify support, and so instead of just a few hundred students who were there most of the time, two and a half thousand turned up, because they didn't think there should be student victimisation." Even so, by the weekend fractures were emerging: for some the point had been made and it was time to withdraw. The Evening Mail even ran a piece on 'How we rallied the moderates: the inside story of the efforts of four students opposed to the sit-in'. Support also splintered along departmental lines: when a vote was held to determine whether to continue, the engineering department cancelled classes so students could vote to bring it to a close.

Added to this was the fact of fatigue. "We were all pretty whacked by the end of it," recalls Phillips. At the extraordinary general meeting that moved to finish the sit-in, Tyrrell remembers how R T Jones, the Guild's Permanent Secretary, and his deputy Frank Jewes counted the votes of the 4,000 students gathered: "we came up with the idea that we would use the arches in the building in front of Big Joe, and the 'ayes' would go to the left, and 'nos' would go to the right." It was with handheld clickers, then, rather than with batons or tear gas, that the sit-in ended. Like the campus clock-tower itself though, one question still looms large over the whole affair: what did the sit-in actually achieve?

The Legacy

For certain members of faculty, the consequences were harsh; sociology lecturer Dick Atkinson, who had led the sit-in's more militant fringe, failed to have his contract renewed. On the student front, though, Phillips is fairly upbeat: "we were able to challenge the status quo in an organised and, I would argue, effective way. We were able to express a lot of the ideas we had through activities. We were able to develop really good working relationships with the faculty." Still, for students who were hoping to radicalise the institution, the results must have been disappointing. Change was gradual rather than revolutionary, the sit-in not really bearing fruit until a few more years down the line. In Durbin's words, students eventually "did sit on committees - by the time I was Guild President in '71, at least we had a mechanism for a voice."

As the first female president, Durbin's election was indeed an advance on the male-dominated character of the sit-in, which reflected Birmingham University's broader inequalities. As Wickham notes, "about five sixths of the university population was male. It was before Germaine Greer and the women's lib thing got going. So, you know... it was quite traditional." It's also fair to see the event as parochial, an institutional squabble that turned dramatic because of administrative ineptitude and a peculiarly restive student body. The university has changed dramatically in the last 50 years, with current students numbering just shy of 30,000, the old library demolished to make way for greenery, and the inside of the Guild refurbished beyond recognition.

And yet – could similar actions happen now? Tyrrell strikes a cautiously optimistic note: "I think there is a need for students to recognise what went before them," to see "what previous generations of students did, partly to enable them to be doing what they're doing now." In 2013 the Defend Education campaign saw students occupy the Aston Webb building like their forebears. The university responded far more punitively this time around, namely with injunctions, suspensions, and arrests. Reasons for rebellion have changed in the intervening years, but they have not gone away. If 1968 can teach today's Birmingham undergraduates anything, it's that a courage to speak up can sometimes win the day. Well, that and the Vice-Chancellor forgetting to shut his window.

Cover of the Birmingham Post, 6 December 1968

MIRACLES TAKE A LITTLE LONGER

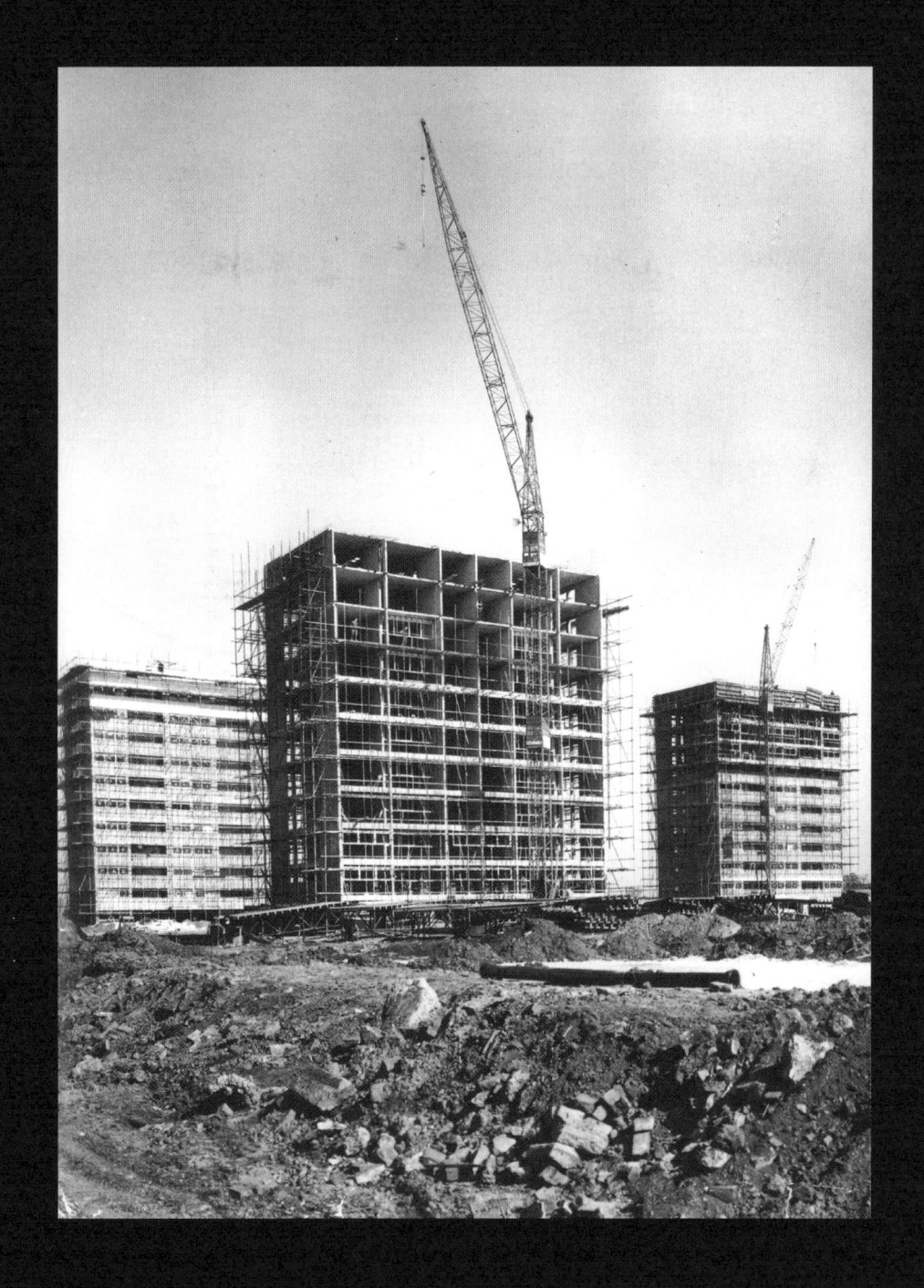

The early 1970s saw the culmination of Herbert Manzoni's vision. After more than a decade of demolition and rebuilding, the new inner ring road was opened by Queen Elizabeth on 7 April 1971. The following year the Aston Expressway and Spaghetti Junction were unveiled, placing Birmingham at the heart of the UK's new motorway network, and in 1974 John Madin's imposing brutalist blueprint for a landmark Central Library became reality. In a three-year period between 1966 and 1969, over 30,000 new council homes had been built. This was envisaged as the moment when Birmingham would take its place on the world stage as a truly modern city, but the celebrations were tempered by uncertainty. The local economy - fuelled in part by this boom in road-building and construction - was beginning to falter, and discontent with the new housing estates was growing louder. Had Birmingham's bold gamble on the future paid off?

These anxieties are writ large in *Miracles Take A Little Longer*, a 1971 documentary made by Hugh Pitt for BBC Two. It opens at dawn in the grand Victorian streets around Colmore Row. We see a solitary bobby on the beat, and then a milkman. Gradually the streets begin to fill with people. Culturally mixed citizens emerge from maisonettes and tower-blocks to begin their daily commute, and the new underpasses rumble with traffic. The first voice we hear is that of Frank Price, describing the "bloody awful conditions" of his pre-war childhood in Hockley Brook: the shared lavatories, the hand-me-downs, the bed bugs. "I don't understand how people can argue now that they're not better off, because by God we were in a mess."

We move onto the Post & Mail Building, where newspaper editor Frank Owens strides around the office smoking and reflecting on "the inhuman size and complexity of modern institutions... the individual is in danger of becoming a digit, a cipher." This tension between modernity and the individual runs through the film, the narrator himself torn between admiration at the scale of Birmingham's achievements and horror at the potential human cost. "It seems each day that the skyline is altered. Old buildings fall, new ones rise. Roads appear where they have never been before, and the old familiar streets are blocked off or disappear altogether... It is one thing to build a new city, but another thing to persuade people to enjoy it."

Alderman Frank Griffin is drafted in to argue the case on behalf of the city council. (Yes, all of the principal voices in this documentary belong to middle-aged white men called Frank - even the narrator, who is Frank Windsor from *Z-Cars*.) "No city could do more than we've done. No city has ever attempted to do as much as we've done... We provide the homes, the new open areas with the grass and the little trees which will grow into great trees. We believe the people themselves must make an effort to get themselves into a community." There's a tetchy tone to the words of both Price and Griffin: the ingratitude of these people, after all that we've done for them!

However, it was becoming increasingly apparent that people transplanted to the new estates wouldn't just "get themselves into a community". The layout and design of the tower-blocks mitigated against community connection and offered a fertile environment for crime and antisocial behaviour. By the late 1960s council waiting lists for high-rise accommodation had plummeted as people increasingly rejected flats in favour of houses - not just because of the disconnection, but because problems were emerging with the buildings themselves. In July 1967 tenants of the new Druids Heath estate reported recurring issues with damp, the first of many such complaints which were compounded by the cold, wet winter of 1968. It became clear that during the industrialised building process used to produce these blocks, the construction company had left insufficient time for the concrete to dry out.

That company was Bryant, who a few years previously had been a medium-sized local building firm. The rapidity of their growth throughout the 1960s was remarkable, fuelled by a virtual monopoly on council contracts for high-rise housing. During the 1950s they received approval for just over 300 flats, while the following decade this figure was close to 10,000. Of the £30 million in high-rise tenders awarded by Birmingham City Council between 1964 and 1968, over £25 million went to Bryant. This was in part due to the speed and (apparent) efficiency of the Bison block system, responsible for a significant majority of the 30,000 dwellings completed during that period, but that was not the only reason for Bryant's supremacy in the Birmingham housing market.

Between 1966 and 1973 Birmingham's City Architect was Alan Maudsley, responsible for overseeing an unprecedented explosion in council housing completions. Like Bryant he had risen quickly, from a junior planning position at Leeds City Council to a role with significant autonomy, multi-million-pound budgets and eye-watering housing targets. In 1970 he was awarded a CBE for services to local government, but in late 1973 he was arrested on a corruption charge along with Evan Ebery and James Sharp, two local architects in private practice. The following summer the three defendants faced 31 charges, and during the trial it emerged that Maudsley had received a Mercedes, exotic holidays and substantial bribes from the pair in exchange for council contracts totalling over £1 million. All three entered guilty pleas and were given prison sentences between eighteen months and two years, and during summing-up Sharp's QC declared that the case was "just the tip of the iceberg". Sure enough two Bryant executives were

Previous page:
Construction of tower blocks at Castle Vale (Bryant, 1965)

Right: Alan Maudsley
(Birmingham Post, 1976)

Next page:
Left: Balsall Heath Road and Cox Street West
Right: Clevedon Road
(Mike Jee, 1970)

"The work was out of this world. We were living like millionaires. We were in the golden era. A new city had absolutely been created. Millions of pounds of work had been put on the market and built, and all the professional people of the city had enjoyed a part of it - me a very large portion of it. But I had to sell my soul to the Devil."

– James Sharp in the Birmingham Post, 1976

THIS WAY TO THE REVOLUTION

MIRACLES TAKE A LITTLE LONGER

later charged with conspiracy to corrupt, the judge on the trial describing Birmingham during this period as a "municipal Gomorrah".

Joe Holyoak graduated from architecture school in 1968 and his first job was in Maudsley's office. He remembers the corruption being "common knowledge... Alan Maudsley and Jim Sharp had matching cars with adjacent number plates." At the same time, this was a gravy train with very tight budgetary constraints. There's no doubt that the department achieved a phenomenal output in the late sixties, and the cost of council housing remained significantly lower than in other parts of the UK. "Maudsley ran a fantastically efficient machine," says Holyoak, "he did the job that his political masters asked him to do."

Herbert Manzoni died in Birmingham in 1974. With time many of his developments would fall victim to the neophilia which he himself espoused, modernist buildings rejected just like their Victorian counterparts a generation before. Architect John Madin, a central figure in Birmingham during the 1960s and 1970s, would outlive many of his own creations including the Post & Mail Building and Central Library. Of the 464 tower-blocks constructed during the high-rise boom, less than half are still standing with many more scheduled for demolition.

Frank Owens' words are acccompanied by images of oil paintings and sculptures in the Museum & Art Gallery, towards the end of *Miracles Take A Little Longer*. Amidst the upheaval and uncertainty of the present, the film is looking to youth for some clue as to the future - even if the youths aren't actually asked for their opinion.

> "This isn't a barbarous, uncivilised city, but of course there's much more that we have to do. I believe... that we will have a sort of cultural renaissance in Birmingham - and I say this because I'm much excited and stimulated by the critical good taste that is shown by our young people today."
>
> – Frank Owens

We see riders from "the famous Double Zero club" on their way to yet another funeral, and then segue to Cannon Hill Park. "The Hell's Angels are also welcome at the less spectacular and more sedate Midlands Arts Centre... The scheme has so far cost three quarters of a million pounds, and the Centre hopes to spend as much again to complete it."

In fact the Midlands Arts Centre nearly collapsed under the weight of its debts in the summer of 1971, and had to be bailed out by the Arts Council and local authority. The more ambitious elements of John English's plans would never be realised, and press criticism of the place was growing by this point. In a piece for The Observer the following year headlined 'Middle class ghetto', Judith Cooke talks about the disgruntlement expressed by some former employees, and a perception among local families that the place is "too posh for them."

The MAC would survive, shifting its model away from "socially divisive" membership fees, but this period was a testing time for many of the utopian endeavours which had sprung up in the previous decade. David Collyer would soon leave the Double Zero and the coffee bar would become a hostel, scattering DZ members to the four winds. Mothers and Henry's Blueshouse had both closed their doors by 1972. Birmingham Arts Lab hung on through crisis meetings and regular cashflow emergencies, eventually establishing itself as one of the region's key arts organisations.

Meanwhile, the collective fervour of student protest had given way to the mundane slog of politics. In the wake of the occupation, University of Birmingham authorities may have neutralised any genuine threat to the status quo, but the events of late 1968 continued to create ripples. As we've seen, one of the occupiers went on to become the Guild's first woman president, a big deal on a campus where the Guild bar had operated a men-only policy just ten years previously. Catherine Hall and a number of other female Great Hall veterans would play an integral part in the first local flowerings of the women's movement in the early 70s, and soon afterwards the university would also become a focal point for the Gay Liberation Front in the Midlands.

Occupation tactics helped to shape the changing face of student volunteering too, with Balsall Heath continuing to play a symbolic role. In February 1969 - while the media was getting agitated about nude performances at the MAC - two thousand Birmingham University students took part in a 'Community Action Week' with interventions ranging from a "discotheque for paraplegics" to a "hostel for dossers and vagrants" in Balsall Heath. Three months later two students dismantled a campus exhibition on housing problems and reassembled it in an empty council house in Knutsford Street, Balsall Heath. Having been ordered to return the photographs forthwith, one of the protagonists Gerald Hitman pronounced the action a success: "the attention of slum dwellers has been drawn to the complacency of the City Council, and the large amount of adverse publicity might well shake the corporation into a more honest appraisal of its housing policy."

Throughout the following autumn and winter living conditions in the neighbourhood continued to make the headlines of Redbrick, with a number of students actively supporting a Balsall Heath rent strike. When the council pulled out of a planned debate with some of these activists along with local residents and Arts Lab members, chair of the housing committee Alderman Beaumont-Dark was suitably dismissive: "I suppose young people will always think they are experts on anything." The demolition of the area around Clevedon Road had been scheduled for 1971, but the furore stirred up by the strike helped to bring this forward a year. Just before everything was flattened, Cadbury employee Mike Jee followed in Janet Mendelsohn's footsteps and documented the condemned terraces block by block.

University people would remain strongly involved in the area as the new Balsall Heath began to take shape. Pam Cook and Alan Barr, who had founded Student Community Action as Birmingham undergrads in 1969, took an office at St Basil's with help from David Collyer, and then set up a community drop-in centre in a derelict house on Vincent Street. Around the same time Dick Atkinson's salary as a sociology lecturer was being paid by his colleagues - after he was effectively blacklisted by the university for his role in the occupation - and he decided to leave academia behind for community development work. As Balsall Heath Forum's Chief Executive Atkinson would become a vocal advocate for the area, travelling some distance from his radical roots. The Forum grew out of the controversial Streetwatch campaign which drove visible prostitution out of Balsall Heath in the early 90s, and was later cited as an inspiration for David Cameron's Big Society agenda.

I CAN'T FIND BRUMMAGEM

In 1965 radio producer Charles Parker held a meeting of local folk clubs to explore the potential for a Birmingham and Midland Folk Centre. The aim of this initiative was to gather, document and perform traditional songs indigenous to the Midlands: as Parker put it at the time, "only if we belong truly to Birmingham or Wolverhampton or Wednesbury can we belong to England." One of their first discoveries was a woman in her eighties named Cecilia Costello, a font of local songs who shared her repertoire on tape. Soon afterwards the group started the Grey Cock Folk Club, named after one of Mrs Costello's more lurid numbers, and by the end of the sixties they had compiled sufficient material for a book of songs and a record, released by Topic as *The Wide Midlands*.

One of the stand-out songs on the album is a ballad by music hall entertainer James Dobbs, first performed at the Theatre Royal on New Street in 1828. Written from the perspective of a traveller returning to the city after twenty years away, 'I Can't Find Brummagem' describes the disorienting effects wrought by rapid industrial expansion in the early 19th century. It's no surprise that the song's lyrics resonated with a 1960s audience reeling from a decade of redevelopment.

The Wide Midlands (Topic, 1970)

Full twenty years and more are passed
Since I left Brummagem.
But I set out for home at last
To good old Brummagem.
But ev'ry place is altered so
Now there's hardly a place I know
Which fills my heart with grief and woe
For I can't find Brummagem.

As I was walking down the street
As used to be in Brummagem,
I knowed nobody I did meet
For they've changed their face in Brummagem
Poor old Spiceal Street's half gone,
And Old Church stands alone
And poor old I stands here to groan
For I can't find Brummagem.

But what's more melancholy still,
For poor old Brummagem,
They've taken away all Newhall Hill
From poor old Brummagem,
At Easter time girls fair and brown,
Came rolly-polly down,
And showed their legs to half the town,
Oh! the good old sights in Brummagem.

Among the changes that abound
In good old Brummagem,
May trade and happiness be found
In good old Brummagem.
And tho' no Newhall Hill we've got
Nor Pudding Brook nor Moat,
May we always have enough
To boil the pot in Brummagem.

James Dobbs (1781-1837)

ENOCH POWER

One unexpected consequence of the storm around 'Rivers of Blood' was a spate of reggae tunes directed at the man who gave the speech. A few months later Laurel Aitken recorded 'Run Powell Run': "We don't want no hostility, we're just begging you for equality." In its wake came Latin-themed number 'The Bull' by Freddie Notes and the Rudies - with Freddie cast as the matador, and Powell as the bull - and then 'Enoch Daughter', a slightly lewd reverie set in a Birmingham motel which appeared as a white-label B-side by Lloyd Coxsone. Perhaps the most life-affirming of the bunch is 'Enoch Power' by Millie Small, which appropriates the politician's name for an anthem about unity.

Small is still best known for her break-out bluebeat hit 'My Boy Lollipop,' released in 1964 shortly after she came to the UK as a Jamaican teen sensation. In the early 1970s the singer stopped recording and performing altogether and has given very few interviews since. Thanks to some dogged detective work by one of our volunteers - and maybe because she was delighted to be asked about something other than 'Lollipop' - we were able to set up a short phone conversation with Millie Small about the story behind 'Enoch Power.'

The singer came from humble origins in Clarendon, Jamaica, the daughter of a plantation overseer and one of twelve kids. Winning a Kingston talent contest gave her a first taste of fame, and once she had relocated to London, Island Records head Chris Blackwell began grooming her for stardom. One of her first overseas gigs was in Birmingham in 1963, a place which still holds fond memories for her: "It had a nice mix of people - Indian, Chinese, West Indian and all of that. It's a nice little spot." After 'My Boy Lollipop' went to number 2 in the UK and USA things would never be the same again, an international success which offered a first taste of Caribbean music for many listeners and paved the way for countless other ska and reggae musicians. Small released a wide array of singles and EPs in the years that followed, but nothing that would match that early explosion.

Recorded in 1970 for Trojan Records, *Time Will Tell* marked a change of direction from the 'girl next door' Millie with a cover photo which featured her skimpily dressed and straddling a massive banana. The LP's contents, however, were far more thoughtful than the packaging suggested: "*Time Will Tell* is the best thing I've done - a damn good album" believes the singer. Produced by German painter Eddie Wolfram, her partner at the time, and garnished with strings by Nick Drake's arranger Robert Kirby, the first single was a cover of Drake's melancholy 'Mayfair' which Trojan paired with the more upbeat 'Enoch Power.' "It was supposed to be called 'Enough Power,'" remembers Small, "but my manager suggested I use 'Enoch Power.'" Imagining a multicultural West Midlands dancefloor, perhaps inspired by those early 60s gigs, the lyrics are a wry riposte to Powell's apocalyptic rhetoric. Undoubtedly it resonated with black audiences at the time, and Small was asked to sing it at Wembley stadium in 1970 as part of the landmark Caribbean Music Festival. Filmmaker Horace Ove included the performance in his documentary *Reggae*, cutting it together with footage of Powell's speech.

Soon afterwards Small called time on her music career to focus on motherhood, painting and a quieter life. A few years later she had an unexpected encounter in Sloane Square. "I was going to collect my daughter from school, and I saw this man walking towards me - he's about five foot something. I looked at him and he looked at me, and it was Enoch Powell. He looked very, very sad, and I felt sorry for him. He was burning up inside, under all this pressure of hate in him." When I ask her about parallels between 'Rivers of Blood' and Brexit, she is having none of it: "England is much, much better now than when I came here first. I wouldn't live anywhere else, my love."

I arrived from Kingston Town
And now live at the Bull Ring
Got to go to Wolverhampton
Help my brothers do a thing
They work all week
To keep the British country running
Weekend it's reggae time
And the neighbours find it funny
So we all sing

Enoch, Enoch, Enoch Power, Lord, Lord
Enoch, Enoch, Enoch Power
Enoch, Enoch, Enoch Power, Lord, Lord
Enoch, Enoch, Enoch Power

The kids all stomp their boots so much
The dance floor's really shaking
They're having fun then going Dutch
I feel my poor heart aching, so we all sing

Enoch, Enoch, Enoch Power, Lord, Lord
Enoch, Enoch, Enoch Power
Enoch, Enoch, Enoch Power, Lord, Lord
Enoch, Enoch, Enoch Power

One day there'll come a time
When all men will be brothers
They'll talk as well as dance
And live and love with each other
And they'll all sing

Enoch, Enoch, Enoch Power, Lord, Lord
Enoch, Enoch, Enoch Power
Enoch, Enoch, Enoch Power, Lord, Lord
Enoch, Enoch, Enoch Power

Enoch, Enoch, Enoch Power
[repeat to fade]

Lyrics by Millie Small and Eddie Wolfram
Trojan Records, 1970

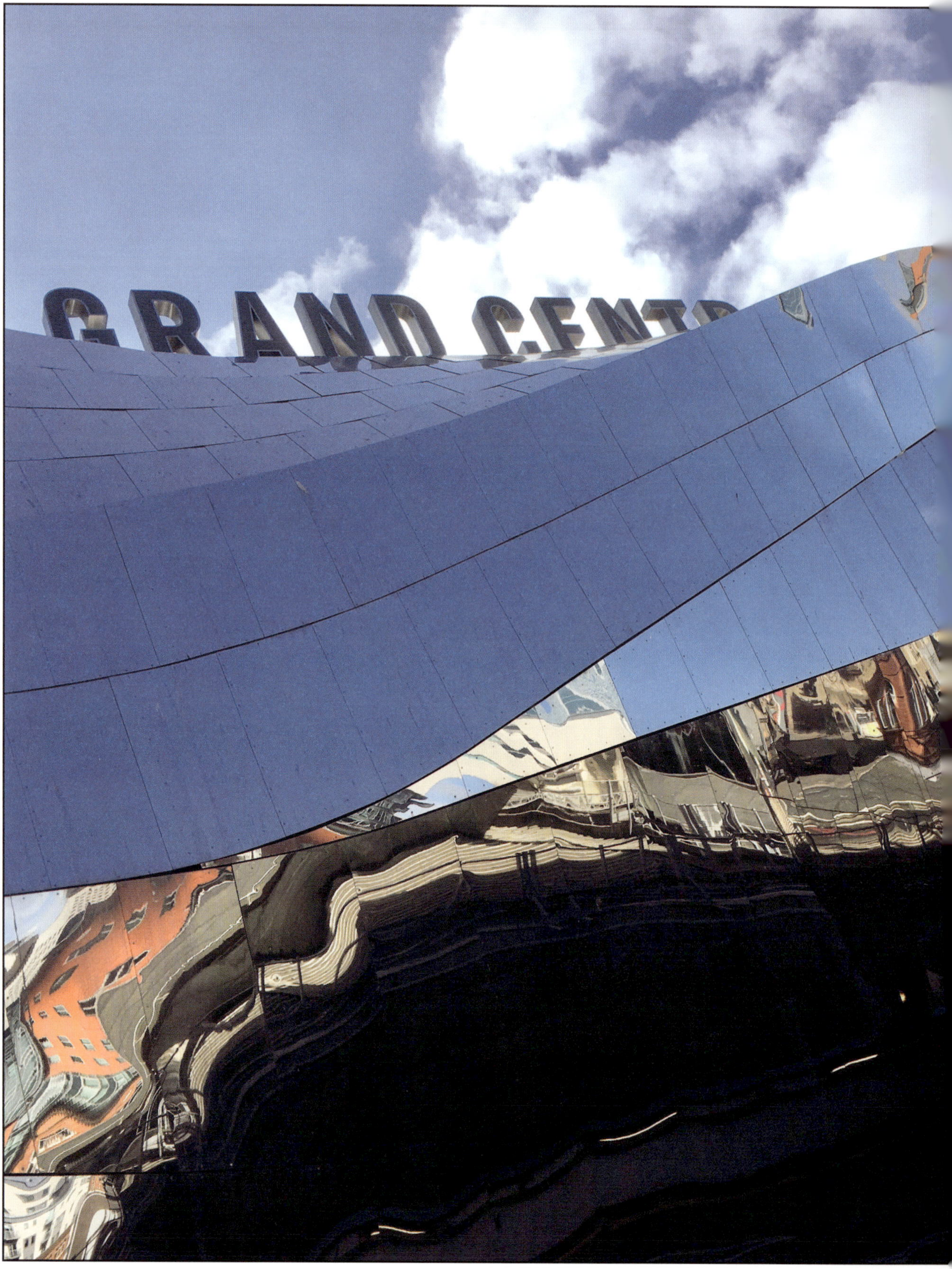
GRAND

FORWARD

The Birmingham 68 project kicks off in April 2018 at the twelfth Flatpack Festival with a weekend stuffed full of exhibitions, screenings, talks and walks across the city. Many of our guests are back here for the first time in many years and are invariably flummoxed on arrival - first by the new New Street station, and then once they've worked out where they are going, by the wholesale change beyond it.

A good chunk of the intervening years has been spent unpicking Manzoni's vision and filling in the unloved pedestrian underpasses which punctuated the inner ring, and since then we have seen the belated second coming of a tram network and a surge in big shiny buildings: the studded blob of Selfridges, followed by the new library and finally the station, covered in angled sheets of rippled metal which reflect back the pedestrians below. Another highrise boom is also underway, but rather than council housing on the periphery this is a wave of 'lifestyle apartments' and student accommodation, part of a plan to repopulate the city centre. Further east a massive patch of land is being cleared in anticipation of a high-speed train terminus which will lop half an hour off the journey time to London, and already south Birmingham house prices are rising as an army of Londoners realise that they can trade in their shoebox flats for a three-bed terrace.

The events programme has the festival team zipping all over the place. At the Electric Cinema in town Graham Williams reflects on leading West Bromwich Albion to an unexpected FA Cup triumph, while in Digbeth Dilip Hiro revisits *Asian Teenager*. In a church in Erdington opposite the site of Mothers - now a Pakistani-run Eastern European supermarket - punters and performers remember a fleeting moment when their patch was the epicentre of rock music, while large crowds of current and former Balsall Heathans converge on the Ort Gallery to see a lost geography resurrected by Janet Mendelsohn's photographs. Sunday is spent largely on foot, firstly through the suburbs of Solihull to trace the origins of industrial music pioneers Throbbing Gristle, and then in the afternoon on a sound walk across the university campus which pieces together reportage and memories of the occupation.

A couple of days later an event at Impact Hub brings together '68 veterans and young activists to reflect on the themes of the weekend. Photographer Vanley Burke, who arrived in Handsworth from Jamaica in 1965 and started using his camera in earnest in 1968, refutes the assumption that his generation were defining themselves against those that came before: "our parents were all we had." He also brings with him some scepticism about the value of 'clicktivism' - the easy

Previous page: New Street Station (Daniel Wright, 2018)

Opposite: Ghost Streets of Balsall Heath at Ort Gallery (Marcin Sz, 2018)

Rajinder Dudrah & Dilip Hiro at the Mockingbird (Katja Ogrin, 2018)

Above: Amerah Saleh and Vanley Burke at Impact Hub (Paul Stringer, 2018)

Below: Double Zero reunion at Mutt Motorcycles (David Rowan, 2018)

option of retweeting or signing an online petition - but declares himself impressed by the passionate commitment of the younger speakers.

Some of those participants go on to join our Birmingham 68 team, meeting soon after the festival to talk through the stories and leads that have emerged and to plan our research. We then disappear down our various wormholes: the music scene, protest movements, race relations, urban planning, motorbikes, photography and so on. Rebecca Took interviews her grandfather Philip about his time as a bouncer at Mothers, Anne Durbin and Chloe Deakin compare notes on feminism then and now, and Ahsen Sayeed records Anil Bhalla's take on the Arts Lab and community action. Interviewees will often caution that they can barely remember a thing. Once they are off and running though, the stories flow like water. "At the time it was just stuff that you did," muses Nick Hedges, "and now it turns out to be history."

During the summer I attend a subcultures conference in Porto to give a paper on the project. For some reason I have been scheduled alongside talks on right-wing nationalist rock scenes in Spain and Poland - perhaps because Enoch Powell was mentioned in my abstract. People seem interested. Maybe this isn't just a Birmingham thing. I expect Black Sabbath to grab their attention, but it's the name Stuart Hall that really makes their ears prick up - he retains rock star status with cultural studies scholars across the world. In the bar afterwards I ask if I need more of a theoretical framework. "Don't worry about that," says a South African academic. "Just tell the story."

In September we link up with Kehinde Andrews from Birmingham City University, launching his book on black activism before a screening of *Black Power Mixtape*. Kehinde's father Maurice was involved in setting up Harambee in Handsworth in the early 1970s, an organisation which provided accommodation for young black men estranged from their families. The same week there's a solo performance at Town Hall by Joan Armatrading, too often omitted from the roll-call of the city's musical luminaries. Born in St Kitts, Armatrading was sacked from her first job at a tool-makers in Hockley for playing her guitar during lunchbreak. By 1968 she was appearing in a touring production of archetypal flower power musical *Hair*.

There is a period in the autumn when a reunion seems to be taking place every weekend. At a university alumni gathering people talk about the apathy of students today. A small band of Arts Lab survivors return to the building on Tower Street, which is now a children's nursery. The women who run the place listen with amusement as respectable retirees reminisce about sleeping beneath the floorboards and smoking weed on the roof. At a motorbike shop in Digbeth a group of Double Zero members gather to swap war stories, their jackets still festooned with patches. One woman spots a glimpse of her recently deceased husband in some archive footage, a young man flying past on his bike.

In October I am at the MAC. The centre still occasionally gets accused of being a 'middle-class ghetto', but it is way more permeable than in John English's day and over a million people go through its doors every year. The focus is no longer exclusively on young people either, and very few in the theatre audience that night are aged under 40. Playwright David Edgar is appearing onstage for the first time in nearly fifty years, presenting a one-man show called *Trying It On* which looks back at 1968 and asks whether his generation of utopian student protesters actually achieved anything. The script's climax has the twenty-something stage manager come out from behind her desk to berate him for pontificating from his expensive house while today's youth are being sold down the river.

The following month Lucy McCormick gives a one-off Club Fierce performance in a drafty warehouse, enacting the story of the New Testament using nubile male assistants, Nutella and all of her orifices. I can't help wondering what councillor Norah Hinks (p32) would have made of it. I also see a shouty hardcore band from Cologne at a cafe in Stirchley, and they are delighted to hear that their fellow citizens nearly got the MAC closed down with nudity and paint-throwing. (At this point I can shoehorn Birmingham 1968 into pretty much any conversation within two minutes.)

By Christmas we have delivered almost everything we promised to the National Lottery Heritage Fund. A plethora of events has happened, over thirty oral histories have been gathered and three podcasts have launched online. This book, however, is nowhere near finished. I have completely underestimated the amount of time that research and writing will take. There is another festival on the horizon, and my colleagues are understandably impatient for me to leave 1968 behind and return to the present day. I negotiate a project extension.

In the new year the exhibitions department at MAC get in touch with a message from a man called Frank Cook. I call the number, and speak to both Frank and Val. They recently celebrated their fiftieth anniversary and are living in the south of France. I am beyond excited, and probably a little over-familiar - although we've never met, I feel I know them inside out through Richard Rogers' pictures. They agree to come over to Birmingham for Flatpack in May.

In February SHOUT Festival mount an event marking fifty years of The Nightingale - yet another ad hoc venture which sprang up in late sixties Birmingham to fulfil a particular need, and still going today. Sick of being ripped off by unscrupulous pub landlords, a group of gay men led by Laurie Williams set up a members' club in an old Indian restaurant in Cape Hill. With Heritage Lottery support, SHOUT plans to tell this story in 2020. A little later I get a letter from the police. The primary school next door to me has become a focal point for protests about LGBTQ education, and an exclusion zone has been established in our neighbourhood.

What are the protest movements we'll remember in 2068? Will it be the feverish dogma of the culture wars, or the climate strikes my son takes part in on a Friday morning? Whereas back then the battleground was employment or housing, today it is identity or the environment, but the rhetoric can be just as divisive - perhaps more so thanks to social media. Drawing historical parallels is a mug's game, but when we looked back at the aftermath of 'Rivers of Blood' the resonances with Brexit were hard to ignore. Both events made visible - and helped

Opposite: Three Birmingham 68 contributors

Steve Ajao with a self-portrait painted in 1968 (Ian Francis, 2018)

Santokh Singh outside Uncle's (Dan Burwood, 2018)

Anne Durbin on the occupation soundwalk (Jack Spicer Adams, 2018)

Below: Home of Metal's Black Sabbath exhibition at Birmingham Museum & Art Gallery (Katja Ogrin, 2019)

to entrench - a huge national rift. It's also notable that like Enoch Powell many in the Leave campaign pinpoint the sixties as the moment when it all started to go wrong for Britain. The loss of deference. The break-up of empire. The decline in manufacturing. The rise in immigration. The permissive society. Feminism. Gay rights. Churchill's funeral.

As we emerge from the festival, musical echoes of 1968 are everywhere. The Beatles' 'White Album' has already been back in the album charts in a Super Deluxe reissue, and "Tuesday is once again Blues Day" as Jim Simpson revives weekly editions of Henry's Blueshouse at a pub in the city centre. Sutton Coldfield Town Hall hosts a fundraising revival of Mothers featuring various stalwarts of the club including Soft Machine, Edgar Broughton and Chicken Shack, and then in June Home of Metal's long-awaited Black Sabbath exhibition launches at Birmingham Museum & Art Gallery.

On the opening day I ride my bike across Balsall Heath, down through the territory which was redeveloped shortly after Mendelsohn mapped it out. Pakistan are playing at Edgbaston in the Cricket World Cup. On every side-street fans with dayglo green wigs and flags are emerging from their cars, while further into the city centre clusters of young back-packers are beginning their pilgrimage to Glastonbury Festival. The exhibition includes plenty of nods to the early years - a Henry's membership card, copies of the underground press, a Mario Bava poster - as well as celebrating the band's global reach.

That afternoon there's an unveiling ceremony for a Black Sabbath Bridge, to complement the Black Sabbath Bench which already sits on Broad Street. On a little island in the middle of the canal basin tribute act Sabbra Cadabra are knocking out the hits while the wind shreds their pull-up banners and metal fans line the towpath. Just as the (suspiciously Mancunian-sounding) Ozzy impersonator launches into "what is this that stands before me?" a narrowboat glides into view bearing the actual Tony Iommi and Geezer Butler along with various dignitaries. Leaving aside the Partridge-esque bathos of the whole thing, it's clear that both of them are touched by the hometown tributes and Iommi is good enough to point out Jim Simpson standing on the bridge: "It's all his fault."

Balsall Heath is bouncing late into the night; car horns and firecrackers and kids playing dhol drums in the park. Pakistan have beaten New Zealand, and they are nipping at England's heels for a semi-final place. The cricket continues at the weekend, with a temporary fan zone set up in Victoria Square for the crunch match between England and India. At least three quarters of those present are supporting India, from kids to old ladies, and the atmosphere is terrific - despite England's eventual victory. I am of course inclined to find signposts to our subject everywhere by this point, but it's difficult not to think of the IWA rally which greeted Harold Wilson in the same square. Thankfully this time the Indians are met with good-natured Barmy Army chants rather than fascist salutes.

In 2022 Birmingham will host the Commonwealth Games. As an arts community and a city we are already fretting about this. Beyond the concerns about what the Commonwealth itself signifies, there's the stage fright that Birmingham can suffer from being in the spotlight. Is it a massive waste of money, for a local authority already up to its eyes in debt? How will we tell our story? Are we just going to embarrass ourselves? This is not necessarily down to a lack of self-belief - we know that there is great stuff going on here. However, creating a coherent narrative out of this city remains as tricky as it was fifty years ago when The International Times pronounced the place "impossible to navigate." It is heartening to hear Martin Green, the man in charge of the Commonwealth cultural programme, acknowledge this incoherence: "if one of our stories is that this place is a bit bonkers, that's fine."

Throughout 1968 there was talk of a 'cultural crisis' in the city, as the Repertory Theatre waited anxiously for confirmation of its new home and the Midlands Arts Centre struggled to maintain fundraising momentum. "What is the use of preparing young people for a golden age of leisure," asked Fred Norris in the Evening Mail, "if they are to grow up in a city which remains, culturally, in the dark ages?" One of the lessons I'd like to draw from this project is that culture in Birmingham is not necessarily where you expect to find it. Few people thought of the Double Zero or the Newtown Palace or the Nightingale or even Mothers as an important part of the cultural scene at this point, but all these places fulfilled a vital need for the people who used them.

They also had in common a certain amount of shrewd bodging, which seems to be part of Birmingham's DNA. The industrial boom which created such rapid growth in the eighteenth century was partly sparked by people improvising workshops in their homes and back yards, and the same spirit is at work in the birth of the Arts Lab through scavenged building materials - or indeed the birth of heavy metal as a genre. This blend of art and pragmatism is reflected in the city's emblem, flanked by a male worker and a female painter and emblazoned with the word 'Forward'. Historically the balance has been fairly lop-sided, with art seen as a bit of decorative garnish, but this has changed. In 1968 manufacturing jobs still accounted for more than half of the city's workforce. By 2017, it was less than 10%, and like many other post-industrial cities we are looking to the creative sector to help fill this hole.

What role the city council might play in this is another question. It's still the largest local authority in Europe, but the bullish days of Joseph Chamberlain and his 'civic gospel' - or indeed 'little Caesar' Harry Watton - are long gone. The reasons are partly financial. Central government cuts have taken a massive toll, and an equal pay lawsuit has cost the city over a billion pounds. The council's staff has halved since 2010, and Birmingham is way ahead of other UK authorities in the race to sell off its assets. There has also been a cultural shift. The kind of grand visions we saw from the postwar planners are unimaginable now, perhaps in part because we're more conscious of the unintended consequences they can have. It's ironic that the boldest scheme on Birmingham City Council's books is

Below: Forward coat of arms in Victoria Square
(Veronika Vlková, 2016)

Opposite: Ghost Streets of Balsall Heath at Ort Gallery
(Marcin Sz, 2018)

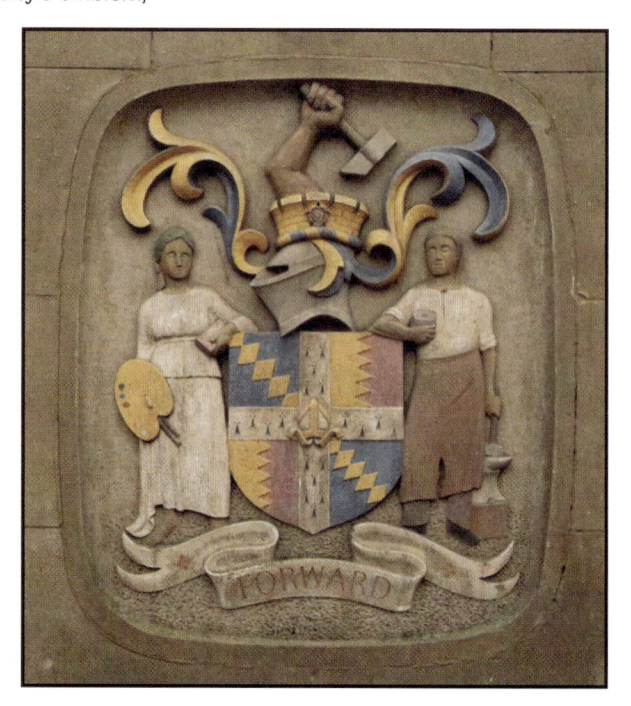

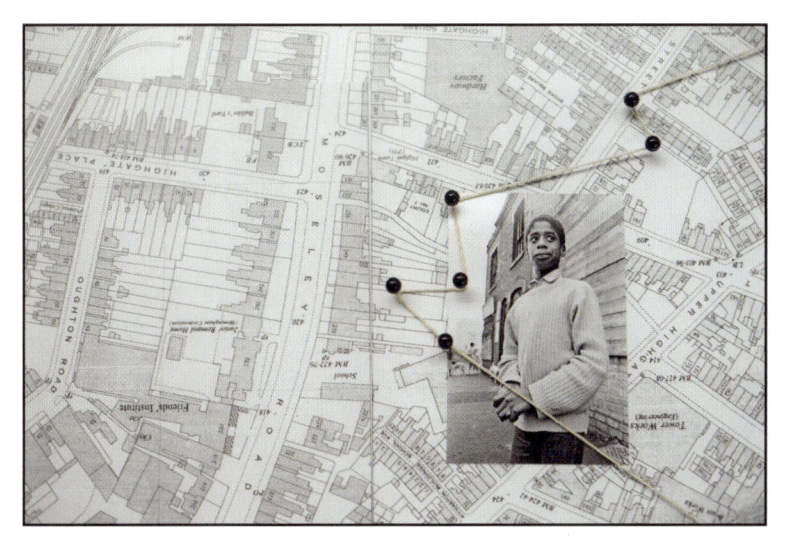

a clean air zone; another attempt to mend the damage done by Manzoni's car-centric revolution.

Shortly before we embarked on this project, Flatpack screened a documentary about the battle of wills between New York's 'master builder' Robert Moses and the writer and campaigner Jane Jacobs. Moses, an avowed influence on Manzoni and Price, wielded prodigious power in his city and pushed through road development schemes which displaced thousands and cut neighbourhoods in half. A believer in the organic development of cities and no fan of cars ("the automobile has been the chief destroyer of American communities"), Jacobs was one of the first to articulate a counter-argument to the postwar planners and managed to halt some of Moses' more radical schemes.

Did Birmingham have a Jane Jacobs? On a small scale you could say it was the Reverend Norman Power, speaking up against blanket redevelopment on behalf of his Ladywood parishioners. As a conceptual corrective to the people-free, bird's-eye symmetry of Manzoni's vision, you could do a lot worse than turn to the work of Stuart Hall. Hall was not particularly interested in urban planning, but he understood the texture of cities and saw that resistance can happen on a microscopic local level - particularly through popular culture. The future which Birmingham thought it was building in the 1960s turned out to be very different, and I would argue that the stories which we've explored in this book played just as much of a part in shaping the city we know today as did the Public Works Department.

A couple of days after the England match, India are back at Edgbaston playing against Bangladesh. As I ride past somebody hits a boundary, and the wall of noise nearly knocks me off my bike. I continue through Cannon Hill Park, past the MAC and up to the university. A Stuart Hall Symposium is taking place in the arts building, marking the return of Hall's personal archive to the site where he first helped to forge a new academic discipline. Hall died in 2014, and some bridge-building has been required to reach this moment; there is still a lot of rancour about the way in which the Centre for Contemporary Cultural Studies was closed down by the university.

Alongside the CCCS veterans giving papers is a younger, more diverse generation of academics. Amanik Saha from Goldsmiths talks about the continuing relevance of Hall's thinking on new ethnicities, and his influence more broadly: "a number of us in this room wouldn't be here if it wasn't for the work he did." Hall's daughter Becky closes proceedings with a moving, funny talk that brings the house down and helps to gently undermine the cult of personality which can accumulate around her dad. She kicks off with her own birth in 1968 - "a few short weeks after a student sit-in, and right in the middle of the Christmas screening of *Some Like It Hot*" - and concludes by reflecting on the return of these documents to the city "where I'm sure Stuart would have been glad to find himself at home."

Epilogue:
FRANK AND VAL

A year after we had shown a selection of 1968 images of Frank and Val Cook at the same venue, I found myself sitting onstage in the Midlands Arts Centre's Hexagon theatre with the couple in the flesh. They had travelled up from France a couple of days before, and half of the audience was made up of their friends and family. For an hour or so we chatted our way through Richard Rogers' photographs, piecing together the story behind a pivotal moment in their lives. Frank began by talking about his first encounter with Richard at the MAC.

Frank: My mum had bought me a camera, and I went to Ladywood where the demolition was going on to take some shots. When I came back I developed the film, and Richard was looking at the images on the enlarger. He asked if he could come back to Ladywood with me the following day and take some pictures, together. We got talking in a pub afterwards, and he more or less said "how about you feature in some of the pictures, I could follow you around a bit and you could be a central thread, you and your wife." So it was like, eight months of him following us wherever we went.

Val: I suppose I didn't really give it much of a thought... he was just someone that was there, and it wasn't intrusive. It was just...wake up in the morning and sometimes he was at the end of the bed!

F: He was coming in on the back of a wave of American cultural high. You know, post-painterly abstraction, the pop-art movement, American music becoming super-duper. He was riding that wave really, and he was full of that confidence. Quite wild hair, lovely smile, nice guy. He used to wear a big combat jacket, with loads of pockets for the lenses and stuff.

Opposite: Frank and Val Cook (Richard P Rogers, 1968)
Below: Frank and Val at the MAC (Asya Draganova, 2019)

Frank had been around Ladywood all his life, first living on Osler Street by the reservoir and later on Alexander Street. Val had grown up in Aston, and met Frank in their teens at a table-tennis match: "the first words he said to me were 'can you tie my shoelaces?'" Having discovered art at grammar school Frank was a keen painter and was tipped off to the existence of the Midlands Arts Centre by his friend the cartoonist Edward Barker. After having his membership approved, Frank took on a small studio space there in October 1967 - just before he and Val got married.

F: It was very middle-class, and to be honest, we did feel a bit out of it really. You still very rarely had a penny in your pocket, that kind of thing. But it served a purpose. Without it I wouldn't have got to Chelsea. You know, I did some good work at the Arts Centre and I met some good people... But I don't think the Arts Centre was designed for really hard-nosed, serious artists who wanted to get stuff done. So yeah, we were a little bit in conflict. You can see why the Arts Lab came along, in a way. Because I think John English's thing was - foreign students coming over every summer, build the amphitheatre, work camps, kiddies coming in and making puppets with jumble, little bits of finger pottery and all that. But obviously you can't control how things want to morph, can you?

It also emerged that Val had been involved in Yoko Ono's 1967 performance in the arena.

V: For some reason we were there, and why she picked on me I have no idea. Apart from the fact that I had longish hair then. She said "oh can you come sit on this chair with your back to the audience" to represent the audience on stage - not that I really understood it at that time. And so I was sat on the stage all the while she was doing, oh I don't know, there was all sorts of little bits of paper floating down with wishes on them, goodness only knows...

By this point the couple had moved into their first home together, a bedsit round the corner from the centre in Oakfield Road. Shortly afterwards Frank's parents also moved to Balsall Heath, one of the last to be cleared out of a rapidly disappearing Ladywood.

Frank and Val at the MAC
(Richard P Rogers, 1968)

F: What was crazy when we were with Richard, is although you'd lived there all your life, you'd come back two days later and...it was just rubble. There was nothing - no features you could recognise. You might as well have been on the moon really... I think the town planners after the war had decided - wisely or unwisely - to destroy the area and rehouse. But what they didn't realise - alright yeah, the conditions are unsanitary - but there was still a community there. And basically they would send you to tower blocks, where there were no shops, no cafés, pubs, restaurants. They put people into deserts. It needed doing, but it needed doing differently.

Frank's dad never put down roots in Balsall Heath and would continue to travel back to his old social club every week.

F: Because he'd come from extreme poverty, Ladywood to him was - he said it was great! You know, it was a marked step up. And to have a health service... my Auntie Violet had two children die in a week from diphtheria!

V: I don't think youngsters today really understand, just in the short space of fifty years, how much has changed. From washing in a tin bath to having all mod cons, iPhones and iPads and that sort of thing.

Through Rogers the couple also met Janet Mendelsohn, and Frank would occasionally make prints of her Balsall Heath photographs in the Arts Centre dark room.

F: She was such a waif-like woman, I don't know how she stood her ground in those situations... she got in some scrapes, *because obviously she was dealing with pimps and prostitutes and stuff like that. And there was a lot of threatening, you know, because pimp guys didn't like photographs being taken. But the way she got on with the prostitutes was absolutely amazing. You know, the most lovely photographs coming out of there.*

By the summer of 1968 Frank had an interview at Chelsea School of Art, and it was Rogers who drove him down. Every step of the journey is documented: kissing goodbye to Val, loading artwork into the American's battered Ford Anglia, shaving in the station loos on the morning of the interview. By the time Frank confirmed his place the couple were expecting their first child - Val believes the photograph on the previous page was taken in September, when she was already pregnant. After a successful year at Chelsea, making work partly inspired by the redevelopment he'd seen in Birmingham and London, Frank got work as an assistant to the kinetic artist Liliane Lijn. He also spent some time involved in the Workers Revolutionary Party, although politics and painting didn't mix well: "they said it was a bourgeois thing, and I rebelled against that." Val: "I'd already rebelled, because I always ended up looking after the children at meetings."

Through what he describes as a series of chance encounters Frank ended up with his own building firm, and later a furniture business in Kent. The couple now live in southern France on fifteen acres of property, with children and grandchildren living just down the road. They're delighted with the way that things have turned out, although you can hear a tinge of regret when Frank talks about his artistic practice. Where once his late night painting sessions were a cause of friction, after a couple of heart attacks and a supposed retirement the two of them are nowadays more likely to argue about his inability to stop working.

Towards the end of the discussion we open it out to audience questions. In a moment that might have been choreographed by Cilla Black, a voice emerges from the back row. Frank peers into the gloom: "Johnny Allen!" It's an old friend from George Dixon school who he hasn't seen in over fifty years, and the two of them reminisce about the way their creativity and ambition was nurtured by one particular art teacher, Mr Hanks. A couple of days later we meet up again in a café, to record an oral history which will sit alongside the photographs in the Cadbury Research Library. Frank brackets Richard Rogers with Patrick Hanks as one of those who people who "adds to your confidence... your sense of what you can and can't do." As they're leaving the couple reflect on how little of the Birmingham that they knew is still standing and talk about the exhilaration of being reconnected with that past. "When we first got in contact," says Val "suddenly we're getting all these photographs, and it's like - this is our life! It's been quite a trip hasn't it?"

THANKS

A project like this doesn't happen without an army of people pitching in - whether that be sharing stories, loaning souvenirs, taking photos, hosting events, funding research, digging through old newspapers, spreading the word, offering advice, cataloguing material, designing posters, or a thousand other contributions large and small. It makes me dizzy trying to think of everyone we've worked with over the last couple of years, but I will have a bash...

Most importantly, the whole thing would not have happened without the Birmingham 68 team - in particular our amazing volunteers who brought their own interests and skills to bear on a complex subject, and helped bring history to life with research, podcasts, writing, photographs and events.

Volunteers: Harry Alimo; Matthew Bruce; Nina Conway; Chloe Deakin; Rita Fonseca; Joe Georgiou; Ahsen Sayeed; Rebecca Took.

Jackie Miley was supremely unfazed when knocking our tangled pile of research into a useable shape. Daniel Clifford helped us to compile all the stories into three excellent podcasts which can be found at the Flatpack project page, listed below, and Nita Newman offered useful tips on recording a good oral history. Rico Johnson-Sinclair was a terrific volunteer-wrangler - moonlighting as a silky radio presenter - and project coordinator Jenine McGaughran kept the whole show on the road with enthusiasm and good humour. Invaluable PR and marketing support came from Grace Chapman, Keenia Dyer-Williams and Margaret London. Particular thanks go to uber-volunteer Edward Jackson, who went beyond the call of duty in his research endeavours and ended up not only tracking down Millie Small but also writing two chapters in this book.

A huge range of partners contributed to all the exhibitions and events which took place during Flatpack 2018 and beyond, including: Josie Reichert, Ridhi Kalaria and Rachael Cox (Ort Gallery); Deborah Kermode and Jess Litherland (MAC); John Hall and Chris Ansell (Parkside Gallery); Log Roper (The Framers); Bohdan Piasecki and Bethany Slinn (Free Radicals); Ben Waddington (Still Walking); Asif Afridi (brap); Bobbie-Jane Gardner and Janette Bushell (ForWards); Scott Johnston (Film Ficciones); Annie Mahtani (Sound Kitchen); Linzi Stauvers and Jonathan Watkins (Ikon Gallery); Faisal Hussain (True Form Projects); Izzy Mohammed (Future Seed); Matt Moore (MJM Bespoke); Keith Dodds; AG Photographic; Kehinde Andrews (BCU); and Sam John Jones (Mutt Motorcycles).

Once the archival digging began in earnest, a vast jigsaw of tip-offs and useful conversations helped to move things forward. Research support has come from Paul Long and Rajinder Dudrah (BCU); Ed Barlow (BBC); Clare Watson and Phil Leach (MACE); Jez Collins (Birmingham Music Archive); Lisa Meyer and all at Home of Metal; Miles Glendinning (Edinburgh University); Tom Graves; Pam Bishop; the Archives and Collections team at Birmingham Library; Sandra Hall (Friction Arts); Adam Carver (SHOUT); Roger Shannon; David Grindrod; Ralph Smith; Linda Spurdle (Birmingham Museum & Art Gallery); David Edgar; Bob Blizard; Kerrie Holland; Paul Willis; Sarah Wilson; Schalk van der Merwe (aka the 'South African academic'); and Angela Lloyd. Laser-guided proofing was courtesy of Lucy Reid.

Kieran Connell (Queen's University Belfast) can take some blame for instigating the whole thing by bringing Janet Mendelsohn's photographs back to the UK, and Josh Allen was very open in sharing findings from his own HLF project, Activist Selly Oak. Helen Fisher (Cadbury Research Library) has been receptive and helpful throughout, and the oral histories and a selection of the material we gathered can now be found at CRL (along with extensive materials on the occupation and CCCS). Thanks to all those who loaned us visual material for the book (see over), and to all the brilliant photographers who let us use their work - especially David Rowan, who captured a mountain of ephemera for us. We owe an enormous debt to Nick Hedges, Janet Mendelsohn and her partner Marc Levitt, for allowing us to use a wealth of images which tell us so much about Birmingham at that time. It has been a pleasure comparing notes with Susan Meiselas as she pursued her own parallel nerd quest, and Susan and her team have been exceptionally generous in giving us access to Richard Rogers' work.

None of the above is much use without a story to tell, and the biggest joy of this project has been sitting down with people and diving into their memories of Birmingham at a crossroads moment. I am generally resistant to sixties nostalgia, but talking to many of our interviewees it has been hard to escape the sense that this was a pretty special time to be young. Even if sometimes the stories they had to share were painful, in each case their honesty and willingness to give their time was humbling. Contributors included: Catherine Hall; Val and Frank Cook; Ian Gorin; Bob Groves; Steve Ajao; Jenny Baines; Julie Beckett; Graham Willams; Dilip Hiro; Affie Jeerh and Gurdip Kaur; Peter Thompson; Lawrence Byrne; Kafait Shah; Santokh and Surinder Singh; David Collyer; Barbara Haywood; Ray Fox; Peter Stark; Simon Chapman; Tony Jones; Mark Williams; Anil Bhalla; Terry and Lyn Grimley; Bob Linney; Ernie Hudson; Stuart Rogers; Peter Walsh; Syd Wall; Robert Moore; Philip Took; John Taylor; June Nichols; David Darkes; Graham Holyoak; Jim Simpson; Norman Hood; Nick Hedges; Avtar Singh Johal; Ian Evetts (aka Spydeee Gasmantell); Anne Durbin; Chris Tyrrell; John Butcher; Jenny Wickham; Ray Phillips; Joe Holyoak; Vanley Burke; and Millie Small.

Special thanks go to our funders the National Lottery Heritage Fund, and especially Olivia Hall for her patience and understanding while we dragged this book over the line. Additional support came from Flatpack's principal funders the British Film Institute, Arts Council England and Birmingham City University.

I owe several pints to the Flatpack team and trustees who put up with me living in 1968 for two long years - notably Abbe Elliston, Sam Groves, Amy Smart and Poppy Gilbert. Props to designer Justin Hallström for his intuitive grasp of the project and a supernatural ability to make everything look good, and to my parents for imparting the value of persistence, passion and pedantry. Finally, all of my love and thanks go to Asya Draganova - for editorial nous, and for bringing the revolution.

Ian Francis

Director, Flatpack Projects
flatpackfestival.org.uk/projects/birmingham-68

Birmingham 68 contributors and team members. Left to right: Matt Bruce; Joe Georgiou; Edward Jackson; Ahsen Sayeed; Rico Johnson-Sinclair; Ben Waddington; Bobbie-Jane Gardner; Jackie Miley; Ian Francis; Annie Mahtani (Greg Milner, 2018)

IMAGES

Cover *Victoria Square rally* (Nick Hedges, 1968)
Inside front cover *Tower blocks in Nechells Green* (Nick Hedges, 1968)
Inside back cover *Rotunda by night* (Nick Hedges, 1967)
8 *Rotunda cartoon* (Wormzy, Birmingham University Guild Handbook, 1968)
11 *The New Birmingham* (Frank Price, Birmingham Public Works Dept, 1960)
13 *Gravelly Hill Interchange* (Melissa Price, 2016)
19 *Janet Mendelsohn and Richard Rogers* (Richard P Rogers, 1968 - courtesy of Susan Meiselas)
20 *Catherine and Stuart Hall* (Richard P Rogers, 1968 - courtesy of Susan Meiselas)
Campus map (CCCS Annual Report, 1966-67)
21 *Alexander Street, Ladywood* (Richard P Rogers, 1968 - courtesy of Susan Meiselas)
Clevedon Road, Balsall Heath (Janet Mendelsohn, 1968 - courtesy of Cadbury Research Library)
23 *Frank and Val Cook* (Richard P Rogers, 1968 - courtesy of Susan Meiselas)
25 *Miscellaneous images of Birmingham* (Richard P Rogers, 1968 - courtesy of Susan Meiselas)
26-29 *Images of the Midlands Arts Centre* (Richard P Rogers, 1968 - courtesy of Susan Meiselas)
30-31 *Promotional leaflet* and *scale model* (Midlands Arts Centre, 1972/1965)
32 *Perception Weekend with Yoko Ono* (Midlands Arts Centre, 1967)
33 *The Scene That 'Shocked' The City* (Redbrick, 26 February 1969)
34 *Life drawing class* (Richard P Rogers, 1968 - courtesy of Susan Meiselas)
Ajao family Christmas (1958 - courtesy of Steve Ajao)
36 *1971 King Lear puppet by Joye Beckett* (David Rowan, 2018 - courtesy of Jenny Baines)
Conflict programme cover (Festival Arts, 1969 - courtesy of Jenny Baines)
37 *Festival Arts at the Garden Theatre* (Festival Arts, 1969 - courtesy of Jenny Baines)
38 *Dilip Hiro* (unknown, c.1959 - courtesy of Dilip Hiro)
41 *Charles Parker at Keele Folk Festival* (Brian Shuel, 1965)
42 *Mohammed Mossadeq* (Asian Teenagers, BBC 1968)
45 *Work Is A Four Letter Word poster* (Universal Pictures, 1967 - illustration by C Bruce Steffenhagen)
46 *Ironic street sign at Free Balsall Heath Festival* (Nick Hedges, 1969)
48 *Janet Mendelsohn at Small Heath Fair* (Janet Mendelsohn, 1968 - courtesy of Cadbury Research Library)
49-53 *Images of Balsall Heath* (Janet Mendelsohn, 1968 - courtesy of Cadbury Research Library)
53 *Site That Has Angered A City* (Birmingham Post, 12 September 1968 - courtesy of Trinity Mirror)
57 *Ray Fox and friend outside the Double Zero* (unknown, c.1969 - courtesy of Ray Fox)
Rev David Collyer (unknown, 1966 - courtesy of David Collyer)
58 *Inside This Jacket Is A Citizen - Double Zero fundraising leaflet* (1967 - courtesy of Ray O'Connell)
59 *Cover of Double Zero by David Collyer* (Fontana 1973)
Double Zero members jacket (David Rowan, 2018)
63 *Advert for Strange Days II* (Redbrick, 9 October 1968)
64 *Arts Lab fundraising image* (unknown, 1968 - courtesy of Simon Chapman)
Arts Lab membership card (designed by Simon Chapman - courtesy of Peter Stark)
65 *We Need Your Bread fundraising poster* (the high peering one, 1968 - courtesy of Peter Stark. Photograph by David Rowan, 2018)
66 *Building in Birmingham fundraising brochure* (design by Roger Street, 1969 - courtesy of Peter Stark)
67 *Arts Lab launch flyer* (1969 - courtesy of Peter Stark)
68-69 *Images of Birmingham Arts Lab* (Simon Chapman, 1969-1971)
70 *Artslabmen membership poster* (Bob Linney, 1973 - courtesy of Bob Blizard. Photograph by David Rowan, 2018)
72 *Mike Westbrook Brass Band with Newtown kids* (Tony Jones, c.1970)
73 *Mothers membership card* (courtesy of Syd Wall and Birmingham Museums Trust)
74-77 *Mothers ephemera 1969-1971* (courtesy of Syd Wall - photographed by David Rowan, 2018)
76 *Mothers audience member* (Birmingham Evening Mail, 1969 - courtesy of Trinity Mirror)
78 *Rev Gary Davis at Henry's Blueshouse*

(Norman Hood, 1971)
80 *Henry's Blueshouse advert*
(December 1968 - courtesy of Jim Simpson)
Black Sabbath
(Jim Simpson, c.1969 - courtesy of Havill Travis)
81 *Henry's Blueshouse T-shirt*
(c.1968 - courtesy of Jim Simpson)
82 *Big Bears Ffolly advert*
(1969 - courtesy of Jim Simpson)
Big Bear Ffolly news cutting
(1969 - courtesy of Jim Simpson)
83 *Big Bear Follies poster*
(Aston University, 1970 - courtesy of Pat Myhill and Home of Metal)
84 *Three images of Locomotive, 1965-1969*
(courtesy of Jim Simpson)
85 *Cover of Jo Sago by Tea and Symphony*
(Harvest, 1970)
87 *Nick Hedges portrait*
(Maggie Gathercole, 1967)
88 *Constitution Hill and the Rotunda by night*
(Nick Hedges, 1967)
90-91 *Caribbean jazz quartet at the Cross Guns, Handsworth* (Nick Hedges, 1966)
92 *Newtown Palace cinema* (Nick Hedges, 1967)
93 *Tower blocks in Nechells Green*
(Nick Hedges, 1968)
Mr Sar and his sons at bathtime in Balsall Heath (Nick Hedges, 1968)
96-97 *Images of anti-racist rally in Victoria Square* (Nick Hedges, 1968)
99 *Who Is Enoch Powell? campaign leaflet*
(Indian Workers' Association, 1968 - courtesy of Avtar Singh Jouhl)
101 *Newtown Palace cinema*
(Nick Hedges, 1967)
102 *Occupation vote* (FW Rushton, 1968 - courtesy of Cadbury Research Library)
104 *Occupation - Tonight! cover* (Redbrick, 27 November 1968 - photograph by David Rowan)
105 *Shabby Treatment flyer* (1968 - courtesy of Cadbury Research Library. Photograph by David Rowan, 2018)
108 *This Way To The Revolution sign* (1968 - courtesy of Chris Tyrrell and Cadbury Research Library. Photograph by David Rowan, 2018)
109 *Cover of the Birmingham Post* (6 December 1968 - courtesy of Trinity Mirror)
111 *Construction of tower blocks at Castle Vale* (Bryant, 1965)
113 *Alan Maudsley* (Birmingham Post, 1976 - courtesy of Trinity Mirror)
114-115 *Images of Balsall Heath* (Mike Jee, 1970)

119 *Cover of The Wide Midlands*
(Topic Records, 1970)
121 *Enoch Power label* (Trojan Records, 1971)
122 *New Street Station* (Daniel Wright, 2018)
124 *Ghost Streets of Balsall Heath at Ort Gallery* (Marcin Sz, 2018)
Rajinder Dudrah and Dilip Hiro at the Mockingbird (Katja Ogrin, 2018)
125 *Amerah Saleh and Vanley Burke at Impact Hub* (Paul Stringer, 2018)
Double Zero reunion at Mutt Motorcycles
(David Rowan, 2018)
126 *Steve Ajao with self-portrait*
(Ian Francis, 2018)
Santokh Singh outside Uncle's
(Dan Burwood, 2018)
Anne Durbin on the occupation soundwalk
(Jack Spicer Adams, 2018)
127 *Black Sabbath exhibition at Birmingham Museum Art Gallery* (Katja Ogrin, 2019 - courtesy of Home of Metal)
128 *Forward coat of arms* (Veronika Vlková, 2016 - courtesy of Mareva Conservation)
129 *Ghost Streets of Balsall Heath at Ort Gallery* (Marcin Sz, 2018)
130 *Frank and Val Cook* (Richard P Rogers, 1968 - courtesy of Susan Meiselas)
131 *Frank and Val at the MAC*
(Asya Draganova, 2019)
132 *Frank and Val at the MAC* (Richard P Rogers, 1968 - courtesy of Susan Meiselas)
135 *Birmingham 68 team* (Greg Milner, 2018)
137 *Girl with camera* (Janet Mendelsohn, 1968 - courtesy of Cadbury Research Library)

Note: Janet Mendelsohn and Richard P Rogers began their projects in late 1967, but as their negatives are undated all images are labelled as being taken in 1968.

Girl with camera (Janet Mendelsohn, 1968)

FURTHER READING (AND VIEWING)

Building The City of The Future
'Going Up Country' (The International Times no.82, 3-16 July 1970, p11)
Frank Price, *The New Birmingham* (Birmingham Public Works Committee, 1960)
Frank Price, *Being There* (Upfront, 2002)
Anthony Sutcliffe & Roger R. Smith, *Birmingham 1939-1970* (Oxford University Press, 1974)
Clair Wills, *Lovers and Strangers: An Immigrant History of Post-War Britain* (Penguin, 2017)

Two Americans in Birmingham
Quarry (dir: Richard P. Rogers, US 1970, 13 mins)
Danny Lyon, *Bikeriders* (MacMillan, 1968)
'Two Views of Birmingham' in Alta: The University of Birmingham Review (Vol 2 No 8, Spring 1969, p67)
Kevin Lynch, *The Image of the City* (MIT Press, 1960)
John Rex & Robert Moore, *Race, Community and Conflict: A Study of Sparkbrook* (Oxford University Press, 1967)
John Berger & Jean Mohr, *A Fortunate Man: The Story of A Country Doctor* (Allen Lane, 1967)
Dhani Prem, *The Parliamentary Leper: A History of Colour Prejudice in Britain* (Metric Publications, 1965)

One Kind of Life
'High Art and the Mind Benders' by Alan Shuttleworth (Mermaid, Spring 1967)
The Pacemakers: John English (Central Office of Information, UK 1969, 13 minutes)
'Black Country Blues' by Bradley Martin Jr - aka Mark Williams (International Times no.69, 5-17 December 1969)
Perception Weekend with Yoko Ono (1967 brochure, MAC archive)
'Be-in was beautiful - then row started' by Colin Smith (Birmingham Post, 16 October 1967)
Tony Robinson, *No Cunning Plan: My Story* (Pan Macmillan, 2016)
'The Scene that 'Shocked' the City' (Redbrick, 26 February 1969)
'International Student Drama Festival: Report prepared by John English and Leslie Holloway, February 28 1969' (MAC archive)

Steve Ajao
John Swift, *An Illustrated History of Moseley School of Art* (An Machair Press, 2004)

Festival Arts
Louise Palfreyman, *Once Upon a Time in Birmingham: Women Who Dared to Dream* (Emma Press, 2018)

Asian Teenager
Asian Teenager 1968 radio script, plus audience response and news cuttings (Charles Parker Archive, Library of Birmingham)
'The Young Asians of Britain' by Dilip Hiro (New Society, 1 July 1967)
Dilip Hiro, *Black British White British* (The Book Service, 1971)
'The Town That Has Lost Its Reason' by Dilip Hiro and John Heilpern (The Observer, 14 July 1968)
Man Alive: Asian Teenagers (Prod. Ivor Dunkerton, UK 1968, 50 mins)
Strangers in a Town (Dir: Philip Donnellan, UK 1969, 50 mins)
A Private Enterprise (Dir: Peter K Smith, UK 1974, 78 mins)

Work Is a Four Letter Word
Henry Livings, *Eh?* (Methuen, 1965)
Work Is a Four Letter Word (Dir: Peter Hall, UK 1968, 93 mins)
'Excuse me dear, don't I know you?...' by Gillian Thomas (Birmingham Planet, 9 February 1967)

Ghost Streets of Balsall Heath
Kieran Connell, Matthew Hilton & Val Williams, *Janet Mendelsohn: Varna Road* (Ikon Gallery, 2016)
'Race, Prostitution and the New Left: the Postwar Inner City through Janet Mendelsohn's Social Eye' by Kieran Connell (History Workshop Journal, Spring 2017, pp 301-340)
'The men who want justice - and a site' (Birmingham Post, 12 September 1968)
The Travelling People (Charles Parker Radio Ballad - broadcast in 1964, issued on CD by Topic Records in 2008)

Less Than Nothing
David Collyer, *Double Zero: Five Years with Rockers and Hell's Angels in an English City* (Fontana, 1973)
Paul E. Willis, *Profane Culture* (Routledge, 1978)
Mary Morse, *The Unattached* (Pelican, 1968)
Tony Palmer, *The Trials of Oz* (The Book Service, 1971)

This Is Our Lab - Let's Not Get Busted
'Building in Birmingham'
(Birmingham Arts Lab, 1969)
Tessa Sidey & Terry Grimley, *Birmingham Arts Lab* (Birmingham Museum & Art Gallery, 1998)
David Curtis, 'London's Two Arts Laboratories 1967-71' (2018, unpublished)
'How YOUR cash is being used to finance hippy "art"' (The Daily Mail, 16 March 1970)

Mothers Days
Kevin Duffy, *Mothers: The Home of Good Sounds 1968 - 1971*
(Birmingham Library Services, 1997)
Laurie Hornsby, *Brum Rocked On!*
(GSM Bestsellers, 2003)
John Taylor, 'Mothers Booking Diary'
(courtesy of Birmingham Music Archive)
'Midlands Movement' by Mark Williams
(International Times no.41, 4-17 October 1968)
Letter by John Taylor (International Times no.43, 1-14 November 1968)

The Big Bear Ffolly
Jim Simpson, *Don't Worry 'Bout the Bear*
(Brewin Books, 2019)
Black Sabbath cuttings file
(courtesy of Big Bear Music)

The Birmingham Inner Circle
Nick Hedges, *the night bus and a country mile: Photographs 1965-1968* (Blurb Books, 2012)
Nick Hedges, 'Photographer's Notes'
(1972, unpublished - courtesy of the author)
'My best shot' by Andrew Pulver
(The Guardian, 2 December 2009)

Black and White Unite and Fight
Birmingham Anti Vietnam Protests
(ATV 16mm rushes, 5 May 1968 - courtesy of Media Archive for Central England)
'Who Is Enoch Powell?' and other assorted papers (Indian Workers' Association collection at the Library of Birmingham)
Kenneth Newton, *Second City Politics: Democratic Processes and Decision-Making in Birmingham* (Oxford University Press, 1976)
'Denmark has got it wrong' by Boris Johnson
(The Telegraph, 6 August 2018)

The Journey Back
Abdullah Hussein, 'The Journey Back' (trans. Muhammad Umar Memon) in *Stories of Exile and Alienation* (Oxford University Press, Karachi, 1998)

Occupation Tonight!
Eric Ives, et al, *The First Civic University: Birmingham, 1880-1940* (University of Birmingham Press, 2000)
'The Student Role' (University of Birmingham Guild of Students, 1968)
Ray Phillips, 'Re-membering the 1968 Birmingham Sit-In' (2003, unpublished)
Chris Tyrrell, 'Reminiscences of Chris Tyrrell' (2018, unpublished)
Redbrick student newspaper (1968-70)
Mermaid, University of Birmingham Magazine (Vol 37, Issue 3, 1968)

Miracles Take a Little Longer
Miracles Take a Little Longer
(dir: Hugh Pitt, UK 1971, 48 mins)
Patrick Dunleavy, *The Politics of Mass Housing in Britain, 1945-75: Study of Corporate Power and Professional Influence in the Welfare State* (Clarendon Press, 1981)
Miles Glendinning & Stefan Muthesius, *Tower Block: Modern Public Housing in England, Scotland, Wales and Northern Ireland* (Yale University Press, 1994)
John Boughton, *Municipal Dreams: The Rise and Fall of Council Housing* (Verso, 2018)
'Corrupt architects sent to prison' (Birmingham Post, 22 June 1974)
'The moral flaws behind Birmingham's modern face' (The Times, 18 May 1978)

Forward
Kehinde Andrews, *Back To Black: Retelling Black Radicalism For The 21st Century*
(Zed Books, 2018)
Norman S Power, *The Forgotten People: A Challenge To A Caring Community*
(Arthur James, 1965)
Citizen Jane: Battle For The City
(dir: Matt Tymauer, USA 2016, 92 mins)

INDEX

A
activism — 10, 11, 12-15, 16, 22, 40, 43, 89, 94-99, 102-109, 116-117, 120, 125, 126, 128, 129
Ajao, Steve — 34-35, 126, 135
Armatrading, Joan — 125
arts funding — 28, 60, 64, 65, 67, 70, 116, 128
Asian Teenager — 10, 12, 38-43, 124
Aston University — 12, 22, 70, 83
Atkinson, Dick — 104, 109, 117

B
Bachdenkel — 31, 66
Baines, Jenny — 37, 135
Bakerloo — 80, 82, 84
Balsall Heath — 10, 16, 21, 22, 24, 25, 27, 46-53, 66, 67, 85, 87, 89, 93, 114-115, 117, 124, 127, 132
Barker, Edward — 31, 32, 131
Beatles, The — 15, 108, 127
Beckett, Julie — 37, 135
Bell, Steve — 70
Big Bear — 78-85
bikers — 10, 20, 24-25, 54-61, 116, 125-126
Birmingham Arts Lab — 14, 16, 25, 31, 32, 62-71, 75, 84, 116, 117, 125, 128, 131
Birmingham City Council — 11, 28, 35, 53, 98, 99, 112-117, 128-129
Birmingham College of Art — 22, 89
Birmingham Evening Mail, The — 11, 13, 76, 99, 108, 112, 116, 117
Birmingham Museum & Art Gallery — 70, 85, 116, 127
Birmingham Post, The — 31, 53, 70, 109, 112, 113, 117
Birmingham Repertory Theatre — 37, 70, 128
Black Power — 15, 40, 43, 98-99, 125
Black Sabbath — 14, 16, 60, 66, 76, 80, 82-85, 125, 127
Black, Cilla — 44-45, 133
blues music — 14, 35, 78, 80, 84, 85, 116, 127
Bowie, David — 63, 84
Bryant Homes — 31, 112-116
Burke, Vanley — 24, 124-125, 135
Byrne, Lawrence — 50, 135

C
Carlton Ballroom, The — 12, 16, 63, 74
Castle Vale — 31, 60, 111
Centre for Contemporary Cultural Studies, The — 16, 19-24, 129
Clevedon Road — 16, 21, 48, 51, 115, 117
Colosseum — 14, 77
Cook, Frank — 16, 22-24, 26, 28, 35, 126, 130-133
Cook, Val — 22-25, 126, 130-133
Crace, Jim — 66

D
Digbeth — 10, 16, 35, 56, 61, 124, 125
Donnellan, Philip — 43
Double Zero — 16, 24, 25, 54-61, 66, 116, 125, 128
Durbin, Anne (née Naylor) — 104, 108, 109, 116, 125

E

Earth - see Black Sabbath	
Emerson, Hunt	70
English, John	28, 30, 31, 32, 60, 63, 116, 126, 131
Erdington	16, 28, 63, 74-76, 124

F

Fairport Convention	75, 76
Festival Arts	32, 36-37
film	15, 16, 20, 24, 31, 43, 44-45, 63, 64, 66-67, 78, 84, 92, 100-101, 120, 129
Flatpack Festival	10, 43, 48, 61, 124, 126, 129
Fleetwood Mac	14, 74, 75, 76
folk music	39, 40, 43, 80, 118-119
Fox, Ray	56, 60, 61, 135

G

Griffiths, Peter	11, 16, 89, 98, 128
Grimley, Terry	66, 68, 70, 135

H

Hall, Catherine	20, 48, 116, 135
Hall, Peter	44
Hall, Stuart	12, 20, 22, 24, 39, 41, 125, 129
Haywood, Barbara	56, 61, 135
Hedges, Nick	24, 46, 86-93, 96-87, 101, 125, 135
Henry's Blueshouse	14, 78-81, 85, 116, 127
Hiro, Dilip	38-43, 124
Hoggart, Richard	20
housing	11, 20, 31, 35, 46-53, 60, 61, 89, 93, 98, 112-116, 117
Hussein, Abdullah	100-101

I

Ikon Gallery	24, 28, 70, 134
immigration	10-11, 12, 13, 15, 20, 22, 35, 38-43, 48-52, 85, 89-93, 94-99, 100-101, 120-121, 124, 125, 127
Indian Workers' Association, The	11, 13, 94-99
international influence	10, 11, 12-15, 19, 20, 22, 28, 32, 35, 40-43, 60, 95, 100, 103, 129
International Times, The	9, 63, 64, 75

J

Jethro Tull	75, 84
John, Elton	75, 84
Jones, Tony	25, 64, 66, 68, 70, 135
Jordan, Colin	11, 95, 98
Journey Back, The	100-101

K

King, Dr Martin Luther	12, 99

L

Ladywood	10, 16, 20, 22, 24, 34, 35, 44, 48, 93, 129, 130, 132
Led Zeppelin	14, 75, 84
light shows	63, 64, 67, 74, 80

INDEX

Lijn, Liliane — 133
Locomotive — 80, 82, 83, 84
London — 13, 22, 39, 40, 44, 56, 63, 64, 75, 84, 87, 89, 120, 124, 133

M
Madin, John — 112, 116
Manzoni, Herbert — 8, 11, 112, 116, 117, 124, 129
Maudsley, Alan — 112-116
Meiselas, Susan — 24, 135
Mendelsohn, Janet — 16, 18-24, 46-53, 87, 117, 124, 127, 132-133, 135
Midlands Arts Centre, The (MAC) — 14, 16, 22, 25, 26-35, 37, 44, 60, 61, 63, 116, 126, 128, 129, 130-132, 134
Mothers — 12, 16, 24, 63, 72-77, 78, 84, 116, 124, 125, 127, 128
music — 12, 14, 15, 16, 25, 28, 31, 35, 37, 40, 63, 66, 67, 72-85, 90-91, 116, 118-121, 124, 125, 127

N
New Street Station — 13, 122-123, 124
Newtown Palace — 89, 92, 101, 128
Nightingale, The — 126, 128

O
Ono, Yoko — 31, 32, 131
Ort Gallery — 50, 52, 124, 129, 134
Ove, Horace — 120
Oz — 61, 63

P
painting — 22, 23, 28, 32, 35, 51, 120, 128, 130, 133
Paris — 13, 35, 89, 103
Parker, Charles — 12, 39-43, 53, 118
Partition — 39, 101
Peel, John — 14, 75, 76, 77, 80, 84
Phillips, Ray — 32, 103, 108, 109, 135
photography — 16, 20-25, 28, 35, 46-53, 80, 86-93, 117, 124, 126, 130-133
Pink Floyd — 74, 76, 77
Plant, Robert — 14, 75
Powell, Enoch — 11, 13, 22, 43, 95, 98, 99, 104, 120, 125, 127
Price, Frank Sir — 11, 28, 112, 129
prostitution — 22, 48, 117, 132

R
race relations — 11, 13, 15, 16, 20, 40-43, 89, 94-99, 120-121, 125, 127
radio — 10, 12, 38-43, 44, 53, 84, 118, 134
Redbrick (student newspaper) — 33, 48, 64, 104, 108, 117
redevelopment & urban planning — 10-11, 13, 19-22, 31, 35, 40, 44, 48, 51, 60, 63, 66, 80, 86-93, 99, 110-117, 118-119, 122-124, 128-129, 132, 133
reggae, ska — 80, 84, 120-121
Ring Road, Birmingham Inner and Middle — 10, 11, 22, 53, 93, 112, 124
Robinson, Tony — 32
Rogers, Richard P. — 18-25, 26, 28-29, 34-35, 126, 130-133, 135

S
Shah, Kafait — 51

Simpson, Jim	78-85, 127, 135
Singh Jouhl, Avtar	16, 98-99, 135
Singh, Santokh	52, 126, 135
Small Heath	28, 31
Small, Millie	120-121, 134, 135
Smethwick	11, 16, 80, 89, 98
Spaghetti Junction	13, 63, 112
Sparkbrook	20, 89, 93
Spirit	74, 75
St Basil's	16, 56-61, 117
Stark, Peter	63-70, 135
Strange Days	14, 25, 63-64, 75, 84

T

Taylor, John	74, 75, 135
Tea and Symphony	80, 82-84, 85
television	43, 44, 55, 60, 64, 97-98
Took, Philip	75, 125, 135
traveller community, the	24, 25, 39, 43, 53
Tyrrell, Chris	103, 104, 108, 109, 135

U

University of Birmingham	15, 16, 19, 20, 22, 24, 32, 60, 102-109, 116-117, 125, 129

V

Varna Road	22, 24, 48
Varty, Suzy	70
Victoria Square	13, 16, 89, 95-98, 127
Vietnam War, the	12, 20, 37, 43, 60, 89, 95

W

Warner, David	44-45
Watton, Harry	53, 128
West Bromwich Albion FC	13, 124
Who, The	76
Wickham, Jenny	104, 108, 109, 135
Williams, Mark	25, 63-64, 75, 135
Wilson, Bishop Leonard	56, 61
Wilson, Harold	13, 95, 98, 128
Wolverhampton	12, 28, 43, 118, 121
women's movement	13, 14, 48, 70, 109, 116, 127
Work Is A Four Letter Word	16, 44-45

X

X, Malcolm	11, 16, 98, 99

Y

youth drama	31, 32-33, 36-37, 44